KU-739-396

OUT OF THIS WORLD

Out of This World

Worldliness and the Christian

JOHN F. BALCHIN

KINGSWAY PUBLICATIONS
EASTBOURNE

ISBN 0 86065 249 1

Cover photo: Spectrum Colour Library

KINGSWAY PUBLICATIONS LTD
Lottbridge Drove, Eastbourne, E. Sussex BN23 6NT
Typeset by Nuprint Services Ltd, Harpenden, Herts.
Printed and bound in Great Britain by Collins, Glasgow.

Contents

Preface

This book started life as a Lent series at Emmanuel Church, Northwood, Middlesex. Because of this I want to put on record my thanks to the former vicar, Richard Bewes, who encouraged me to publish it; to Mrs Marge Hanse, the church secretary, who typed up the transcripts for me; and to the good people of Emmanuel, who had the patience to listen to me!

JOHN BALCHIN

1. No Fixed Abode

My wife and I were steering our luggage trolley through the Taipei International airport in Taiwan. We were used to immigration procedures, and stood in the queue of passengers off the latest flight with our passports and papers at the ready. It was then that I happened to glance up at the notice over the officials' desk, and for a moment it gave me a jolt, for it read, quite simply, ALIENS. 'I can't be', I thought, 'I'm British!' And then, of course, I realized that, as far as the Taiwanese were concerned, I was as alien as any other foreigner who came through that hall. For all that they might make us welcome, and invite us to look around their interesting island, we did not really belong, as the days that followed demonstrated.

When Peter wrote to his friends in what is present-day Turkey, that is how he described them too. He appealed to them as 'aliens and exiles' (1 Pet 2:11). Jesus was saying a very similar thing when he said that his disciples were 'not of this world' (Jn 17:14). In other words, Christians do not belong here. They are citizens of another kingdom; if you like, they are natives of another country, holding different passports from other people. Although they live out their daily lives with the rest of the world, they are actually as alien as I was when I arrived in Taiwan.

The world

When we speak about 'the world', however, we have to be a little careful. The term is used to translate at least two words in our Bibles, and they do not always mean the same thing.

The first is that old, familiar term 'cosmos'. It is an interesting word because it originally meant something that was an ordered system of things. That is what the ladies aim at with their cosmetics, a word that comes from the same root. For the ancient Greeks, this world seemed to be a well-run and decently ordered affair, and in one sense they were right. In this way we can speak about the world that God made in his wisdom, and that he keeps running and supplied by his power. When Paul, in good Old Testament tradition, told the Athenian Greeks that 'God...made the cosmos and everything in it' (Acts 17:24), they no doubt agreed with him.

It was a short step from speaking about the world as a place to using the term 'cosmos' for the people who live there, the world of men and women. This was the world that God so loved that he gave his Son by sending him into it (Jn 3:16). He lived in that world, rubbing shoulders with men and women, largely unrecognized by them for who he was, yet intent on saving that world (Jn 1:10; 3:17).

For the world of men and women is in a mess. Christians are not the only ones to say that people are not what they ought to be, but the Bible has its own distinct estimate of the problem. Mankind, it says, is fallen.

Together we have gone our own way, become careless about God and his laws, asserting our own independence. That is why, in the New Testament, this word 'world' collects the meaning of the spoilt, fallen, sinful world, the world apart from God. Yet this is the system in which Christians still have to live, a system that is, at heart, hostile to God and evil in tendency.

This is why, for instance, John can tell his Christian friends quite plainly, 'Do not love the world or the things of the world. If any man loves the world, love for the Father is not in him.' He then goes on to list out what he sees in the world as 'the lust of the flesh, the lust of the eyes and the pride of life' (1 Jn 2:15–16). It is fairly obvious that John is not talking here about something nice or neutral. He is using the word in the sense of an evil system that is hostile and dangerous to Christians.

And this was not just John's personal and jaundiced view of life. Jesus had some equally pessimistic things to say about the world of men and women. For example, in the Upper Room, just before he went to the cross, he not only spoke about his disciples as being chosen out of the world, and as not belonging to the world (Jn 17:6, 16), he also spoke about the world's hatred and opposition (Jn 15:19; 16:33; 17:14). He, too, was using the word in this narrower sense of an evil and fallen system.

World and church

In this way, 'world' can be set over against 'church' in the New Testament way of describing things. If world stands for the mass of people who have no time for God and no place for his Son, church means God's people. Unfortunately, this word can conjure up wrong ideas as well, especially in English. It originally meant 'a summoned assembly' or 'an assembled group'. It can actually be found in a purely secular sense like this in the pages of the New Testament. The rioting crowd at Ephesus were an unofficial assembly (Acts 19:32, 39, 41). However, for Jewish Christians it had even greater value. In the Greek translation of the Old Testament which many of them read, it was the word used for God's people, especially those called and redeemed out of the slavery of Egypt on their way to the Promised Land.

In the New Testament, a different kind of deliverance had taken place. Through the cross, people had been brought out of the slavery of sin, and not simply as individuals. They soon discovered that they belonged together. They had been called together by Christ himself, and therefore out of the mass of unbelieving men and women who made up 'the world'.

In some ways, this was a very Jewish manner of dividing up the population of our planet. For them, you were either a Jew, and therefore one of God's covenant people, or a Gentile, and therefore outside this scheme. What the earliest Christian preachers offered to both Jew and Gentile alike was a new arrangement—the New Covenant or Testament—by which anyone could join God's people by putting their trust in Christ and in what he had done for them. But just as previously there had been a sharp dividing line between Jew and Gentile, so now there was an equally clear-cut distinction be-tween church and world. You were either inside or outside the group of God's people.

One of the oldest pictures of the church is that of Noah's Ark. The Ark was a symbol of salvation in a world under judgement. Every creature *in* the Ark was saved; everyone *outside* perished. In a similar way, the church came to be seen like the Ark. You are either in the Ark or in the water, but salvation comes through being in the Ark.

I am not saying that in order to be a Christian you must belong to some particular denomination. We have defined the church as believing people, not ecclesiastical structures. However, the man or woman who has only got an individualistic dimension to their Christianity is missing out a great deal on what the Bible describes as normal Christian experience. From the New Testament point of view, you are either in the church, the company of God's people, or you are in the world—and not just the world that God has made; you are in the fallen world of sinful men and women, a world that comes as naturally under God's judgement as the world of Noah's day.

This present age

The other word in our New Testaments that we sometimes translate 'world' really means 'age' (it is our English word 'aeon'). It arose from looking at the world from the point of view of time and history.

The Jews had their own, clear understanding of time. They divided the whole of history into two sections or ages. They spoke about 'the present age' and 'the age to come'. They also sometimes described these two periods as 'the former days' and 'the latter days'. What is more, they expected this present age to pass away when the Messiah, the promised King, came. The important thing as far as the New Testament is concerned, is that the age to come was Messiah's age.

For when the apostles started preaching the gospel, they announced a startling readjustment in the scheme. They gave us a whole new view of history, which they themselves had learned from Jesus, for they claimed that Messiah had *already* come. Jesus was the promised Messiah, as amply demonstrated by his life, death and resurrection.

But if Messiah had come, then Messiah's age, the age to come, must have also come with him! Hence the latter days had already begun. This means that Christians, those who put their trust in Christ, are spiritually speaking, already living in the new age. They have already, among other things, 'tasted the goodness of the Word of God, and the powers of the age to come' (Heb 6:5).

The very expression 'eternal life' not only signifies 'life that goes on for ever'. Quite literally it means 'life of the age', that is, of the new age. We are told on more than one occasion in the New Testament that we do not need to die physically in order to begin experiencing this life. It happens as soon as we commit ourselves to Christ. In that moment, in Jesus' own words, we pass 'from death to life' (Jn 5:24), and therefore into the life of the age to come.

But you may object that this present age is still going on—and you would be quite right. What we have here and now, since the coming of Christ, is something like an overlap between the two ages. We are still living in the fallen world, in the present evil age, but at the same time, because the Holy Spirit lives in each Christian, we are also living in the age to come. That is why the apostle Paul can speak about Christians as being already dead, risen, ascended and seated in heavenly places in Christ (Eph 2:4–7). Spiritually speaking, Christians are already the other side of death, the grave and judgement. In these terms, they already know a foretaste of heaven.

There are plenty of promises in the New Testament that, one day, this present evil age will finally be wound up, and that this present world will come to an end. This will happen when Jesus Christ returns. Then our faith will become sight, and God will complete the wonderful work he has begun in us by his Holy Spirit here and now. Until that time, Christians are called upon to live in two ages at once, and it is this fact that accounts for a good deal of tension in their lives. For however much people feel at home in this world before they become Christians, once they have given their lives to Christ, they begin to see and realize that the system they have called 'home' is, in fact, fallen and corrupt. It is a system which did not, and does not, acknowledge the claims of God or Christ. It crucified Jesus when he came, and it would crucify him again if it had the chance, and for a very good reason.

The ruler of this age

The New Testament describes the world as being in the power of Satan. He is 'the ruler of this world' according to Jesus (Jn 12:31; 16:11), and 'the god of this age' who blinds the minds of unbelievers, according to Paul (2 Cor 4:4). John tells us that 'the whole world is in the power of the evil one' (1 Jn 5:19). To 'follow the course of this world' is to 'follow the prince of the power of the air', who stands behind every disobedience to God (Eph 2:2).

In other words, the devil controls the way in which fallen men and women live. More importantly, he directs the way in which fallen men and women think. He creates the conditions in which they live and grow, which they imbibe, and which they then reproduce in their conduct. So we mean by 'world', as one scholar once put it: 'all the floating mass of thoughts, opinions, maxims, speculations, hopes, impulses, aims at one time current in the world, which it is impossible to seize and accurately define, being the moral or immoral atmosphere which at every moment of our lives we inhale, and again inevitably exhale'.

As I am a non-smoker, I always know when either family or guests have been in a smoke-filled room or railway carriage. Although they got used to the atmosphere, I can smell it on their clothes as soon as they come into the house. The world is like a smoke-filled room in which we have to live and breathe, and go about our daily business. Before we became Christians, it was normal for us, because it was home to us. But when we came to Christ, God gave us a new ability, by the Holy Spirit who lives within, to sense it as an alien atmosphere. For what the Holy Spirit does, as we have already hinted, is to give us a foretaste of our real home, of heaven itself.

He gives us longings and appetites that will only be fully satisfied in God's presence, and which are only really delighted with the things of God here and now. That is why, when I became a Christian, without anyone telling me that I had to, I *wanted* to go to church and to worship the Lord; I *wanted* to read my Bible and to pray; I *wanted* to share my faith with others. He had given me a whole new set of desires and joys which I never had before. What is more, the old life and the old home—this present fallen world—not only appeared fallen to me, it no longer satisfied me. I became aware of it as it really was, the poisonous atmosphere where spirituality could wither and die, and which wanted to reclaim me as one of its own.

Worldly pressure

For that is the effect of the world. It is always wanting to press you into its mould. Just in the same way that we speak of being 'a child of our time', sharing the outlook, the aims, the ambitions and the values of that period of history in which we live so, in spiritual terms, it is all too easy to take in and to give out non-Christian attitudes and standards, simply because we are living in a fallen world. Just like the air all around us, we are living in an immoral and unspiritual atmosphere that is pressing in upon us all the time. We are at even greater risk today than our forbears were. We are exposed to what we call 'the mass media'—TV, radio, advertising, the glossy magazines and the tabloid newspapers—which can diffuse and disseminate this atmosphere very quickly and very efficiently.

I hope that by now you are beginning to see how important all this is for the modern Christian, if he is going to live out the kind of life he has been called to in this present world. For we cannot opt out. The Corinthian Christians had misunderstood Paul in just this way when he told them not to associate with immoral people: 'not at all meaning the immoral of this world, or the greedy and robbers, or idolaters, since then you would need to go out of the world' (1 Cor 5:10), which is obviously a ridiculous idea for the apostle. Some people have tried. The long history of the monastic movement, with its monks, nuns and hermits, often seeking to escape worldly pressure by quite literally running away from it, is evidence of this. Sometimes those who are living in evangelical communities can do so from very similar motives. It is far easier to be a Christian among Christians, away from the influence of shop, or factory, or office, or school.

But that is not how the New Testament writers saw it. They envisaged the possibility of living out Christian values and standards in the ordinary rough and tumble of everyday life and work. When you stop and think about it, this is quite amazing. When God wanted a people for himself, who would live to the praise of his glory, he did not extract them from the fallen world, and transport them to some unspoilt planet. He took them on as and where they were. His purpose is to make us like his Son while, at the same time, giving us the grace to cope with the insidious pressure of the evil system in which we have to live. That makes it an even greater miracle.

Lights in a dark place

This is how Christians come to stand out from the rest. God does a work in their lives which begins the process of transformation which, one day, will make them entirely like Jesus. No wonder Christ himself described his followers as 'the light of the world', there for all to see, and 'the salt of the earth', there to stop the rot (Mt 5:13–16). For by the Spirit, Christians are able to breathe a different atmosphere, the very breath of heaven itself.

It is not natural for men to live underwater, but they can and do, if they take some of their native atmosphere with them when they go down. In this way the aqualung diver has his own independent source of supply in what would otherwise be a lethal environment. If his air runs out, or if he takes off his face-mask, he drowns. Christians live in this present fallen world on exactly the same principle.

For similar reasons, Christians can expect rough

handling from the world. The lifestyle that God gives you passes judgement on those who are living for themselves, by simple contrast. Whereas some will be attracted by it, others will hate you for it. In this respect, church and world are diametrically opposed. This is why Jesus told his disciples that, when both run true to form, there is inevitable conflict. 'If the world hates you', he said, 'know that it has hated me before it hated you.' And the reason? 'If you were of the world, the world would love its own; but because you are not of the world, but I chose you out of the world, therefore the world hates you' (Jn 15:18–19). Remember that it was the world that put Jesus on the cross. 'The rulers of this age', Paul tells us, 'crucified the Lord of Glory' (1 Cor 2:8). Because of this, when the church is true to her calling, she finds that she is living in a hostile world. 'As he is so we are in the world', comments John (1 Jn 4:17).

No fixed abode

So what with the opposition and persecution of this world, along with its contrary standards and values, I am obliged as a Christian to live out this new life of mine as an alien and an exile. I live with the tension of being in two ages at once. My physical, material, daily life is bounded by this present evil age, which is doomed to pass away, but my ambitions, my guide-lines, my outlook and therefore my behaviour, are all determined by a calling and an experience that will only be satisfied in heaven itself. When Paul wrote to the church at Philippi, he used a picture that would have meant a great deal to them. Philippi, although a town in northern Greece, was not a Greek city like the others the apostle visited in the area. It was a Roman colony. It had been founded and settled years before by the Romans and, in Paul's day, it was a little outpost of Roman privilege and culture. They were proud of their Roman origin and citizenship, even though Rome itself was many miles away. It was to these colonists, now Christians, that Paul wrote 'our commonwealth', our citizenship, that is, 'is in heaven'; or as it has been translated, 'we are a colony of heaven' (Phil 3:20, J. B. Phillips).

In this way, we are like an outpost in an alien world, and that means that we have to be on the watch. We have to see to it that the evil in the atmosphere around us does not seep into our lives and into our churches. To use the picture of the Ark again, it is one thing for the boat to be in the sea; it is quite another when the sea gets into the boat! Then you have problems. The church has to remain in the world. There is no avoiding that. But when the world gets into the church, our difficulties begin.

To change the metaphor, do you remember reading about those intrepid men and women who were dropped behind the enemy lines during the Second World War? Although they made contact with the dedicated resistance fighters, they were in a highly dangerous position. They had to assume that everyone was a threat and potentially hostile. They had to be continually on their guard. One slip, one careless word, and their cover would have been blown. Perhaps we need not look on every unbeliever as the enemy, but we are in a similar position of danger that demands constant vigilance. We live in a world where careless Christians go under.

The problem within

Why is it so difficult to live the lives God wants us to live? Why was it that, even in the tremendous blessing of New Testament times, Christians had to be continually reminded to live lives differently from the rest? It is because there is another principle involved. There is within us, even within those who have been truly converted and who know God's power in their lives, something that is still attracted to the world. We still have an old, fallen, sinful, human nature ourselves. It will be ours until we leave it behind in death. In fact, here and now we will only make spiritual progress as we die to self and sin, and progressively allow the Spirit to control our lives. That is the secret of victory (Rom 6:1–14). That is why following Jesus involves denying ourselves daily, and taking up the cross (Lk 9:23).

But that evil principle within us thrives on the spirit of the age. The atmosphere of the world is life to our fallen, human natures. It is this attraction that spells utter disaster for both the Christian and the church. It was disaster for Paul's companion Demas who, we are told, fell in love with the present world, and deserted the apostle (2 Tim 4:10). 'Friendship with the world', pronounces James, 'is enmity with God. Therefore, whoever wishes to be a friend of the world makes himself an enemy of God' (Jas 4:4). 'If anyone loves this world', wrote John, 'love for the Father is not in him' (1 Jn 2:15). You cannot have it both ways. You cannot enjoy the world *and* Christ, for as Jesus himself reminded us, you cannot serve two masters (Mt 6:24).

This is where worldliness comes in. It is when we profess to belong to Christ while at the same time

living, not only *in*, but *for* this world. Instead of being
'transformed by the renewal of our minds', we are
'conformed to this world' (Rom 12:2). Although Christians in name, we give up the struggle, and live like the
rest.

In many ways this is a very easy thing to do. It is
fairly simple to get in step with the world while still
professing to be a Christian. When you begin to do
what the world does, then the world will tolerate and
accept you. You will feel quite at home in its company.
You will become one of its circle again, but your witness
will be absolutely ruined. Jesus said, 'If the salt has lost
its taste, what good is it?' Only good to be thrown out!
(Mt 5:13–14). Never be taken in by the argument that in
order to win the world you must become like the world.
When Paul, for instance, spoke about identifying with
people in order to win them, it was very clearly on
Christ's terms (1 Cor 9:19–23). Our distinctive witness
as Christians is always our difference from the world,
not our likeness to it. Too many Christians have merged
in with their non-Christian background on the pretence
of witnessing, when all the time they were simply
satisfying their own pathetic, human natures.

In actual fact, such people are spoilt for both worlds.
They cannot enjoy the full blessings of being a Christian
because they are not fully committed to Christ. At the
same time, if they have been born again, they have a
conscience that will not allow them to whole-heartedly
enjoy the fallen world either. It is a miserable existence,
even though they try and convince themselves that
they are getting the best of both worlds. That is just not
possible.

Thou shalt not...

Having said all this, it is possible to be different from the world without necessarily being distinct in a Christ-like way. Too often in the past, Bible-believing Christians, in fear of the world, have given the impression that Christian living was a matter of *not* doing things rather than doing them. The answer to worldliness has sometimes been seen as a set of negatives.

When I was converted some thirty years ago, I was virtually presented with an unwritten, evangelical checklist of things that I could not do now that I was a Christian. In those days, going to the cinema was frowned upon, spiritually minded girls would never wear cosmetics, and you would never be seen at a dance. Drink was positively out, as was smoking, and a good number of other things too. We had a whole, long list of rules and, if we kept them all, we were doing pretty well.

It is obviously true that there have to be negatives. If I am living my life for Jesus Christ, there will be many things that I will not and cannot do if I am to remain consistent. But that is only half the picture. What I do not do is more than balanced by the richness of proving Christ and his power in my daily life. Unfortunately the traditional approach to worldliness not only presented a very negative view of what a Christian was, it reduced what ought to have been Christian vitality to strict and often petty legalism. Christians could easily become people who did not do things—and who were proud of the fact!

A way of thinking

There may have been some very sound reasons for some of the old-fashioned scruples but, in biblical terms, worldliness is a far bigger issue than just going to certain places or doing certain things. It is rather a whole attitude of mind, a way of thinking that reflects the spirit of the godless age in which we live. In practice, it expresses itself as we turn to the things of the world in such a way that they become God's rival, taking his place in our lives.

The tragic aspect of this is that, living in the world as we have to, the process of conditioning is sometimes so gradual and subtle that we do not always recognize it is happening. Nowadays we have the attitudes, standards, views, outlooks and morals of the world flung at us continually through the literature we read, the TV programmes we watch, on our radios, and particularly through advertising. We accept them all unconsciously if we are not careful. Before we know it, we have given way to them, and assimilated them. And then, while professing to be Christ's, we reproduce them in our daily behaviour. We finally reach the point where there is really no difference between ourselves and the rest.

I remember chatting to a missionary once who came home every five years or so. I was asking him how he felt about stepping back into the life of his home country like that. He said, 'The sad thing is that, every time I come home, standards seem that much worse. Sadder still, the church seems just that bit more worldly. It has gone just a bit further down the slippery slope without knowing it.' And that, in a nutshell, is the problem for Christians in the West today. As our society gets more and more atheistic and materialistic, if we are not very careful, the tone of church life will progressively go down with it. We will be increasingly taking our cue from the world. The sea will have got into the boat.

How are we to recognize what is going on? Thank God, we are not unaided. We have the Holy Spirit within us, the Spirit whom Jesus said 'the world cannot receive' (Jn 14:17). It is as we are prepared to learn from him that he gives us the sensitivity and the discernment that we need to recognize the world in all its disguises. He can act rather like a burglar alarm. When the burglar tries to get in, it goes off and warns everyone.

In a similar way, you may be watching a programme on TV, and the Holy Spirit says, 'This is incompatible with your confession of the Lord Jesus Christ.' Or you may be reading a novel, and he has to say, 'This is simply inconsistent with what you know to be true and wholesome.' Of course, you need not listen—you can always turn an alarm off. Or you can let the Holy Spirit do his work, and that means taking seriously those means that he uses to shape our thinking, and to mould our attitudes.

High on the list is God's word. It is as we fill our hearts and minds with the truth of Scripture, as his word 'dwells in us richly' (Col 3:16), that we are not only put on our guard; we begin to think the very thoughts of God himself. When that begins to happen, we begin to see the world in its true colours, and to identify it as the sham and fake that it is. For although customs and culture have changed since the Bible was written, the world at heart is very much the same, as are the devil's tactics. In the following chapters I want to look at what Scripture has to say about various aspects of that world, and at the advice given to God's people as they lived out their lives as aliens and exiles.

2. The Things We Have

One of the more obvious and blatant characteristics of the fallenness of the world in which we have to live is its attitude to possessions. By and large, Western society is based on materialism. Not only have the intellectuals reduced everything to matter, and abolished the things of the spirit, but ordinary people also see life in terms of getting and having. They exist for the things of time and sense, and we see this particularly in their mad pursuit of money, and what money can buy.

No new problem

Although modern Western culture is riddled with this philosophy of life, it is really nothing new. Both Jesus and the apostles had to deal with exactly the same attitudes in their own day. One of Jesus' best-known parables, that of the Rich Fool who pulled down his barns to build greater ones, was prompted by it. Someone had asked Jesus to tell his brother to divide the family inheritance with him. While disowning the duty, Jesus went on to warn his followers: 'Take heed, and beware of all covetousness; for a man's life does not consist in the abundance of his possessions.' Then he

26

told the story of the farmer with the bumper harvest, who was wealthy by the world's standards but spiritually bankrupt as far as God was concerned (Lk 12:13–21).

One of the oldest myths is that human happiness, success and fulfilment is getting, possessing, hoarding and acquiring more and more *things*. Materialism, in this sense, is not new, and yet it is a myth that is still believed in spite of the accrued evidence of centuries to the contrary. In that extremely subtle book, Ecclesiastes, the preacher tried it out, as he seems to have tried out most things, only to conclude that it was all 'vanity and a striving after wind' (Eccles 2:11). There have been many since who have proved the same thing for themselves. Read the stories of those who have been financially successful. They are seldom happy or fulfilled people, even though they may have possessed more than they could ever spend in one lifetime.

In spite of this, the myth that possessions spell happiness is believed by many, many people in England today. It sums up their philosophy of life, that man's true well-being *does* consist in the abundance of his possessions. The wealthy are deemed to be the happy; the man who has got it is the man who has 'arrived'.

Unfortunately there is a modern twist to the myth, and it comes to ordinary people in a new garb. With the rising standard of material living, there is an abundance of personal luxuries around. There are, in fact, so many non-essentials on the market that it becomes necessary for manufacturers actually to condition people to be materialistic in their thinking. That is why advertising is such big business, and it is advertising with a difference. Very seldom is it the unsophisticated 'Buy our Goods' approach of yesteryear. Often it consists of a

carefully planned psychological campaign aimed at
manipulating the way people think. They must come to
the point where they see a product advertised and say,
'I must have it. I *need* it', whether they actually need it
or not.

It is well known among the ad-men that, if there is no
real need for a product, it is possible to create a synthetic
need by advertising techniques. Nowadays, advertisers
are very seldom selling the product they advertise.
Instead, they are offering you happiness, or health, or
social advantage, or sexual prowess, or mother love
under the guise of selling cars, indigestion tablets, beer
or margarine. Next time you watch the TV adverts, ask
yourself what you are really being sold. You will find
that very seldom is it the actual product.

No doubt the ethics of advertising are long overdue
for Christian comment, but that is not the point I am
trying to make here. What concerns me more is that I
am living in a generation that is being quite deliberately
conditioned to discontent. It is being subtly schooled
into wanting things. It is being educated in selfishness.
It is being conditioned to covet.

In Britain we have got the government to put a health
warning on cigarette packets. It really ought to be
written across a good many adverts—and not only
adverts. Some of the quizzes and games on TV are
equally open to this charge. You know the kind of
thing. Everything you can remember flowing past you
on the conveyor-belt in a certain time can be yours, free
and for nothing. And then the wonderful goodies begin
to roll by, the toasters, and the lawn mowers, and the
hi-fi sets, and the electric hair-curlers, and so on.
Frankly, that is sheer materialism. It is part of the ethos
of a society that says, 'to live is to have'. We need a

sticker for our sets that reads, 'Remember the Tenth Commandment'. If you have forgotten what that is, it is simply that it is a sin to covet, to want what you have not got. To retort that 'it's only a bit of fun' probably means that you have already been sucked in. You simply do not realize what is going on.

Wanting more

It could equally be argued that this obsession with possessions lies behind a great deal of industrial unrest. Whether it is the individual greed of the managers, or the collective greed of the workers, it amounts to the same thing. We have all been conditioned to want more than we have. It is certainly demonstrated by the phenomenal hire-purchase debt in our country. It is the reason why the country is living on credit. For a similar reason, gambling is booming. After the Act legalizing betting was passed, in a very short time we had more betting shops than post offices up and down the land. Or what about the anxiety about maintaining standards? Why do so many people try to 'keep up with the Joneses'? We have been told repeatedly, and we believe it, that to have is to live, and to live is to have.

That is why the parable of the Rich Fool is so up to date. It was not wrong for the farmer to have a bumper harvest; nor was it wrong for him to pull down his barns and build bigger ones in which to store it. That was good fortune and wise planning. What was wrong was that, having done this, he said to his soul, 'Soul, you have ample goods laid up for many years. Take your ease. Eat, drink and be merry' (Lk 12:16–19). That was what Jesus called being poor. The farmer had laid up plenty of material things for himself, but he was

spiritually bankrupt. God's word to the man is one of
the saddest in the Bible: 'Fool!' Why? That very night
he was going to die, and he would leave it all behind.
He had thought that he could satisfy and provide for
the needs of his soul with the things of time and sense.
He thought he had a bank balance, when in reality he
would step into eternity poor, wretched, miserable,
blind and naked.

People are still taken in today in the same way. Heap
up as much as you will of this world's goods, you will
still leave it all behind when you go. The story is told of
the good old hymn that begins 'Guide me, O Thou
Great Jehovah...'. Apparently, in one of the earlier
editions, instead of reading 'Land me safe on Canaan's
shore', a misprint came up with 'Land my safe on
Canaan's shore'! There are certainly plenty of people
who would like it to be that way, but it simply is not so.
You make it, you strive for it, you get it, you hoard it,
and you leave it. The things of time and sense belong to
this brief life. If you do not realize their soul-destroying
power here and now, you certainly will afterwards.
What will it be like to hear, as God's welcome, 'Fool'?

Coping with possessions

Is it possible for Christians, with Bibles in their hands
and a long tradition of Christian teaching behind them
that has repeatedly emphasized these points, to fail to
see them? Unfortunately yes. If we are honest, we have
to admit that the water can very easily get into the boat
at this point. In fact, when it comes to material possessions, there often seems little to choose between those
inside and those outside the churches in the West.
Because it has been relatively easy, in recent years, for

Christians in the Western world to live and work with little fear of persecution, it has been possible for them to do very nicely as far as possessions are concerned. In some quarters, where middle-class culture has been equated with evangelical profession, it is almost seen as their right and due.

In a way this is to be expected. As we have said, we cannot opt out of society, and therefore we are as open to its advances as anyone else in our generation. We are confronted with materialistic standards and values every time we open a newspaper, or look at a hoarding, or switch on the TV. All unconsciously, it is quite possible for a professing Christian to be just as hooked on possessions as his non-Christian friends or neighbours. Almost without meaning to, he finds himself caught up in the mad scramble for money, and for the things that money can do for him. He can quite easily find himself equating material prosperity with personal fulfilment, even though he goes to church each Sunday, prays, and reads his Bible.

I have come across Christians who are obsessed with the house, or with the car, and who can talk about nothing else than clothes, or furnishings, or the exotic holiday they are going to have next year. Some are over-concerned about what schooling they can afford to give their children; for others, it is the best food and wine. We damn ourselves quite unwittingly by what we say: 'Darling, we really must have...' or 'If only I could get my hands on....'

A good job?

We see it particularly in the whole business of parent-hood, and what we want for our children. What is the

very best that we can imagine for them for the future?
Do we think to ourselves, 'I hope he gets a good job'?
What do we mean by 'a good job'? We mean a job that is
well paid and that has prospects of promotion and
advancement. It is a job with comfortable conditions,
one that will mean material advantage. When we say
that we want our youngsters to 'do well', and 'to get on
in the world', what we really mean is that our best
ambitions for them are purely material! As Christians,
our one overriding ambition for our children should be
that they should know the Lord, and be found in the
centre of his will for their lives. What they do, or what
they earn, where they live, or go, whether they prosper
in this world or not, are entirely beside the point.

Do you remember that when Jesus told the parable
about the Sower, he spoke of the seed falling among the
thorns that grew up and choked it? In his explanation,
the thorns are the cares, *riches* and pleasures of this life
(Lk 8:14). These are the things that choke the spiritual
life out of us until we become Christians in name only.
Church attenders, identifying ourselves visibly with
the people of God, we become really no different at
heart and in lifestyle from the rest.

Is having wrong?

Before we try to state what the Christian attitude to
possessions ought to be, we need to nail one or two
misconceptions. The first is that it is wrong to have
possessions at all, for that is certainly not a biblical
principle. In the Old Testament, material prosperity
was seen as a sign of God's blessing. In the New Testament, there is no denial of personal possessions.

This is well illustrated by the community experiment

after the day of Pentecost blessing. We are told that, in the early days, Christians set up a common fund, and pooled their possessions. They had everything in common, and they shared out the cash to each person as he or she had need. Having said this, it is plain that this was a purely voluntary affair. We see this in the awesome story of Ananias and Sapphira (Acts 5:1–11). The husband and wife, having sold a piece of property, conspired to give only part of the proceeds to the fund, while making out that they had given everything. But their sin was their lie, not the amount they gave. As Peter told them, 'While it remained unsold, did it not remain your own? And after it was sold, was it not at your disposal?' There was no question about the ownership of the property. It was theirs, just as our possessions are ours. Whether that is the way God made the world, or simply how fallen society works, it appears that he sees nothing wrong with actually having things and calling them our own.

A similar misconception is that it is wrong to have a great deal. Once again, this is not borne out by Scripture. Jesus had wealthy followers who supported him and his friends in their ministry. You will find that two rich men actually buried him. Nicodemus and Joseph must have been quite well off, for they not only provided the tomb, but also the expensive embalming spices that went with it. Discipleship is not a question of wealth or lack of it.

But if this is so, what about the young man who was told to go and sell everything he had (Mk 10:17–22)? He was a would-be disciple, and yet, with all his other virtues, this was the one thing he lacked. That in itself may be the clue to what Jesus meant. In his case, his wealth was standing between him and complete trust, just as ours could. Whatever holds us back from complete commitment to Christ is a hindrance that we must dispose of. In the man's case, it was the acid test of his sincerity. What Jesus was really saying was, 'Do you love me more than your cash?'

Trusting in money

When Christ went on to tell his followers that it was harder for a rich man to enter the kingdom of God than for a camel to go through the eye of a needle (Mk 10:25), he was pointing out the extra temptations that wealth always brings with it. When we have enough and to spare, as most of us do in the West, it is fatally easy to transfer our confidence from Christ to cash. But that is not to say that wealth must inevitably come between a disciple and the Lord, even though we have inherited that idea in a strange kind of double-think in England. The church member may earn a great deal and prosper, but, when it comes to our full-time workers at home or overseas, we often work on the theory that poverty is piety. Keep the pastor poor and he will, no doubt, pray more! After all, as one member once said to me, 'He does it for love, doesn't he?' All of which is a travesty of what we should understand by 'full-time service'.

When you stop and think about it, wealth is a very relative thing. A poor man in Western society would be unbelievably rich in many parts of the Third World. There is a sense in which it is well-nigh impossible to live in the Western world without having a certain amount of this world's goods. Again, our differing circumstances will mean that some will need more and others less. A couple raising a family will be considerably more hard-pressed than a single person with a single person's responsibilities, even though they may actually earn more. Wealth is an extremely difficult thing to quantify, and it will vary from place to place and from time to time. As such, possessions, in and of themselves, are neutral. It is no more godly to possess little than it is to possess much. The poor are not necessarily more spiritually minded, even though they may have fewer obstacles in the way when it comes to trusting God totally.

That was the point of Jesus' teaching. It is so very easy, when we have money, to trust in what we have rather than in the Lord. There is a temptation unconsciously to argue, 'I believe in God and in his provision, so long as there's something in the bank to fall back on if things go wrong.' In fact, in terms of personal experience, some have only learned what it really is to trust, in spite of years of professing Christianity, when things have fallen apart. When the business has crashed, or when they have suddenly found themselves redundant, they have discovered that they had nothing to fall back on—except the Lord. It is then that they have really learned to trust for the first time in their lives.

The love of money

If trusting in worldly possessions is wrong for the Christian, longing for them and loving them certainly is. 'Keep your life free from the love of money', we are told, 'and be content with what you have. For he has said, "I will never leave you or forsake you"' (Heb 13:5). It is the Lord we have to love, not money. Paul gave some very similar advice to young Timothy. He reminded him that 'those who desire to be rich fall into temptation, into a snare, into many senseless and hurtful desires that plunge men into ruin and destruction. For the love of money is the root of all evils; it is through this craving that some have wandered away from the faith and pierced their hearts with many pangs' (1 Tim 6:9–10).

What Paul is saying here is the very antithesis of worldly philoshy. For worldly people, money is the root of all good. Think what you can do with it! Think what you can buy and where you can go! Think of what you can enjoy! But Paul says that this is the way of misery. We are neither to trust our possessions nor to love them. Such love and trust must be reserved for the Lord Jesus, and no one else.

Nor must we serve them. When Jesus spoke about people trying to serve God and mammon (Mt 6:24), it is fairly certain that he was talking about material things. If we are not careful, material things can master us, demanding an allegiance that we owe to God alone. We cannot, therefore, serve God *and* material possessions at the same time. As Jesus said, one master is bound to suffer in the arrangement, and he implied that it would be God.

This is probably why Paul can speak about covetousness as idolatry (Col 3:5). It is fatally possible to put money, wealth, possessions, and material things in God's place, and worship them. It is possible to live for things in the same way that we ought to be living for God. It is possible to try to satisfy our souls with the things of time and sense, and to be as illogical as the Rich Fool who said, 'Soul, you have ample goods laid up for many years...'.

True riches

In the light of what we have said, you can see how some Christians in the past have taken the 'safe' way, and renounced possessions altogether. This may be God's way for some, but it is no more spiritual than attempting to come to terms with material things in the ordinary, daily responsibilities of life. For, although the teaching we have been reviewing so far might seem somewhat negative where money is concerned, there are also plenty of positive principles when it comes to the way in which Christians ought to handle material things.

The first is, quite simply, to recognize that real wealth is spiritual. In the parable, the Rich Fool's problem was that, although he had a hefty bank balance, he was not 'rich towards God'. When you come into an experience of the Lord Jesus Christ, you are brought into a spiritual inheritance that you begin to possess and enjoy here and now by the Holy Spirit. The wealth that God gives us through his Son is described in extreme terms in the New Testament. It speaks about the riches of God's grace 'which he lavished upon us' (Eph 1:7–8). 'What no eye has seen, nor ear heard, nor the heart of man conceived, what God has prepared for those who love him' (1 Cor 2:9). Jesus himself promised his friends that there will be no one giving up anything for his sake 'who will not now in this time receive a hundredfold, houses and brothers, and sisters, and mothers, and children and lands, with persecutions, and in the age to come, eternal life' (Mk 10:30). And so we could go on.

If someone has come into a real experience of the Lord Jesus Christ and the exciting new dimensions that he can give to life, they would not trade it for the whole world. The old hymn summed it up so well:

> I'd rather have Jesus than silver or gold.
> I'd rather have Jesus than have riches untold.
> I'd rather have Jesus than houses or lands.
> I'd rather be led by his nail-pierced hands.

To come to a real and personal knowledge of Christ is the first part of our antidote to the world in this matter. When you know Christ, you know what true riches are. When Paul was writing to Timothy about the love of money, he could also say, 'There is great gain in godliness with contentment.' We are content with what we have, be it little or much, if we know what godliness is all about.

Godliness may seem a rather old-fashioned word these days, but that is because of the conditioning we have all been subjected to. Godliness means knowing God, and the things of God, and the riches of God in Christ. And when you know the Lord like this, then you will know contentment. Paul actually borrowed a pagan word here. 'Contentment' was originally used by the Stoic philosophers to describe someone who was 'self-contained', 'independent', 'unmoved by the shocks and bruises of life'. The apostle employs it with a difference. The Christian is 'self-contained' in Christ. He is not dependent on the things of time and sense, or on the varying fortunes of life, because he has and knows the Lord. That is why the Christian who really proves God in this way will stand out in the crowd. This kind of God-given contentment with what we have is the very opposite of the fever of discontent and covetousness that surrounds us today.

This is why Christians are out in front when it comes to talking about a simple lifestyle. Quite honestly, they can say that they do not need the unnecessary luxuries of life, because they are happy in the Lord. They are in the best position to discover what their true material needs, over against their wants, really are. In fact, because they are Christ's, they become more concerned about giving than about getting.

Good stewards

When you gave your life to Christ, you gave him everything. Those are the terms of discipleship. Jesus has to be Lord. It may be that you will spend the rest of your life working out the implications of his Lordship in practical ways, but they are all implicit in that initial surrender. You come to him on his terms. You are now his.

This means, of course, that nothing that we possess is really ours any longer. This is just one of the lessons in that well-known parable of the Talents (Mt 25:14–30). The master gave his servants cash to trade with while he went away. One day he came back, and asked them how they had done. In the same way, all that we have, not only our cash, but also our time, energies, opportunities and abilities, all belong to him. We have them on trust. This means that our money, like everything else, is not ours to possess, but to *use*.

This is a very important lesson for me to learn as a Christian. I should even feel guilty about having things that I do not really use, because what I have, I hold on trust for him. I have it to use for his kingdom and glory, and one day he will call me to account for how I have used—or misused—it. That is what we call stewardship.

As Jesus taught elsewhere, it is possible to convert our material assets into spiritual assets: 'Do not lay up for yourselves treasures on earth, where moth and rust consume, and where thieves break in and steal, but lay up for yourselves treasures in heaven' (Mt 6:19–21). You do this by using those things that the Lord has entrusted to you for him. What is more, whereas material assets are desperately insecure—the bank rate may go down, the stock market may fail or, at best, you leave it all behind when you die–spiritual assets last for ever. These are the things that will stand to your credit at the great accounting of the Last Day.

When Christ returns and asks us what we have done with our trust, our scale of values may drastically change. What will count then will not be the fact that you run two cars or had a holiday last year in the Bahamas, but how you have converted your earthly assets into spiritual ones.

Practical giving

This will mean that, if we mean business with Christ, sooner or later we will deliberately, responsibly, look at our income and ask the Lord, 'Just how much do you want me to give?' It does not actually tell us in the New Testament how much to donate. In the Old Testament it was a tithe, that is, 10% of one's income. In New Testament terms, proportional giving is still recommended (1 Cor 16:2), and certainly sitting down and seriously thinking through the issue: 'Each one must do as he has made up his mind, not reluctantly or under compulsion, for God loves a cheerful giver' (2 Cor 9:7).

It is not a matter of working out our running expenses and then seeing what might be left over for the Lord. God's portion comes first. When we set that aside, we are often surprised at the way in which the rest goes round.

What we need in this country is some down-to-earth, straight-from-the-shoulder teaching on giving in our churches. When I see Christian ministers fighting hard to make ends meet, or missionaries using their hard-earned furloughs tripping round from church to church touting for funds, it makes me wonder if we have ever learned what being Christ's is all about. It is not that Christians in the West are poor. In many ways, we have never had it so good. It is simply that we have never learned how to give, and that, in turn, reflects on what we call our commitment to Christ. How can anyone give themselves to Christ without giving their money? How can anyone be so illogical as to consider themselves Christian, and yet hold back when it comes to giving? The world has got into the church; the water has got into the boat.

At the same time, such people are missing out on so much. Jesus said that 'it is more blessed to give than to receive' (Acts 20:35). It is not just a plain Christian duty to sit down and say, 'Lord, it's not mine; it's yours. Take it and use it as you will.' It is part of Christian joy. We put our cash at God's disposal; we let him use our homes, our cars, and our furniture, and we discover that he is no man's debtor. In our giving, he gives back to us in a thousand different ways.

From the very beginning, my wife and I agreed that we would run our household on these principles, and we can testify, after nearly twenty-five years, that God has enriched us again and again. For anything we may have given, he has given a thousandfold 'pressed down, shaken together, running over' (Lk 6:38). I only want to share the blessing.

Trusting

In sharp contrast with those who are caught up in the rat-race of modern striving and getting, Christians know that God is their heavenly Father. Consequently they can be sure that he will supply their needs. Jesus' argument in the Sermon on the Mount is simply that (Mt 6:25–34). He tells us to think about the flowers. 'Lilies of the field' is a rather extravagant translation. He was probably thinking about the thousands of tiny flowers that scatter the Galilean hills in springtime, only to be progressively dried up and withered as the summer grows hotter and hotter. God clothes them, and they are prettier than even Solomon was in all his pomp. Won't God look after you?

Or the birds of the air? God looks after those. How much more will he be concerned with your daily needs, if he really is your Father? 'O men of little faith'—what a sad description, and yet how often is it true of us? Why not be logical and trust him? If God is our Father, he is perfectly capable of looking after his own. But there is a condition.

On the one hand, we must not be anxiously chasing after the things we think we need. Jesus tells us that such an attitude is pagan when we have a heavenly Father. On the other hand, we need to get our priorities sorted out. What should we seek first? 'The kingdom of God and his righteousness' and, if we do, then all these *things* will be ours as well (Mt 6:33). Put God first, and the rest—including our material needs—will follow. What you eat or drink or wear is now no longer your problem. It is his, if, that is, you put him and his affairs first in your life.

Does this apply to modern living? Does God know

about inflation and mortgages? He has been looking after his people for thousands of years now, so you might even say that he has a fair amount of experience! Yes, his promises were for all time. They still hold good today. The problem is our lack of faith and commitment.

We find Paul saying a very similar thing to some friends of his: 'My God will supply every need of yours according to his riches in Christ Jesus' (Phil 4:19). But once again, there was a condition, only this time it had already been fulfilled. The Philippian church was one of the few fellowships that sent Paul funds. Paul is now telling them that God is generous with the generous, and that he gives to the givers. He is no man's debtor.

Along with a good number of others in Christian ministry, I can testify to that. There have been times when we have had very little, and yet God has never failed to meet our needs—though often not our wants. He has sometimes supplied them to the penny. For many who have been called to live by faith, telling no one their needs but God, that has been their testimony over many years.

Something different

It is when we get our attitude to possessions sorted out, that we not only come into tremendous blessing ourselves, but we begin to present an unmistakable witness to a money-mad world. We make worldly values stand on their heads.

We were once approached by a good friend who was going abroad, and who wanted to give us his car as a parting present. It was to replace our car which was a very much older model. However, he had another Christian friend who needed a car, but who would not think of accepting his as a gift. So we did a sort of three-cornered swop. He gave us his car; we gave her ours.

During that summer before he left, one of my neighbours came across me touching up the paintwork and putting my car in order. Was I doing it up to sell it, he asked. 'No', I said, 'I'm doing it up to give it away', and I told him about our arrangement. It was such a reversal of the world's way of doing things that he was absolutely stunned.

The world says, 'Get, get, get...'; the gospel says, 'Give, give, give...' and the paradox is that, when we do the latter, we are enriched. And that is our witness to unconverted people whose lives are beset by discontent and anxiety. It demonstrates an alternative lifestyle that can be winsomely attractive. It is a different lifestyle, because it is the lifestyle of another age. It is the lifestyle of the Age to Come. It is what the New Testament calls eternal life.

3. The Way We Think

The way in which people think about the world and about themselves is, in some ways, even more important than the way in which they live. This is because our thinking will inevitably be reflected in our living. The sort of attitudes and ideas that people accept direct or warp the whole pattern of their behaviour. If you want to change people, you have to change the way they think—as many a politician, philosopher, advertiser and social campaigner has proved in the past.

The way of the world

As Christians, we have to live in an intellectual climate that is called 'the wisdom of the age' by the apostle Paul (1 Cor 2:6). So, once again, we are not describing anything that is particularly new. Having said this, in these days when there is so much stress on man's cleverness in terms of scientific and technological advance, the whole subject has taken on a new slant. In the past, when you wanted to speak with authority, you could fall back on what God has said, and on what God demanded. Today, you must back your statements with 'Scientists say...' or 'Specialist opinion is...' or 'Experts affirm...'.

For some years now we have been living through a period of intellectual optimism, although this is fast coming to an end. It has been very widely assumed that, given time and effort, we can not only explore the universe and crack all its mysteries, but we can solve all our human problems as well. This outlook is often wedded to an evolutionary view of the human race. The theory is, of course, that over many aeons, men and women have evolved by chance survival or adaptation from a sort of primeval soup into the upstanding two-legged animals that they are now. It has been one long story of progress in every sense, for the same idea is also applied to the field of moral and spiritual endeavour.

Man, we are told, is ever reaching upwards and pressing onwards, and therefore can expect progress at this level as inevitable. What is to come must necessarily be better than what has gone before. According to this perspective, all that men and women need, to come to these further stages in our development, is the right kind of knowledge and training. In this way, we will all eventually come to see the sweet reasonableness of living together in peace, harmony and mutual well-being.

That is why there has been such an emphasis on what we have called education in the West. It is supposed that, if you educate the next generation correctly, this will lead to social reforms and enlightened policies, which in turn will yield human happiness and a balanced, progressive human society. It may be that some of us are becoming a little sceptical about this article of humanistic faith, for such it is, but whether we like it or not, these ideas are deeply rooted in modern society. A great deal of our educational, social, and even our legal philosophy and policy is based on the idea of the essential goodness of human nature, and the inevitable progress of the human race.

Learned doubts

I will not need to convince most of my readers that old and young often find it difficult to understand one another. Old people are often baffled, not to say appalled, by the younger generation, while the latter have written off the elderly and their ways as irrelevant. Again, this is not new, but it has been exaggerated in recent times by the way in which we have been taught to think, and this is another aspect of today's worldly wisdom.

Most of the older generation, when they went to school, were taught to *accept* what they were told. The teacher had said it, and all they had to do was read, mark, learn and inwardly digest! And that was the end of the matter.

The younger generation, by and large, have not been taught that way at all. We might even say that they have been taught the very opposite, to *doubt*. They are encouraged to question things rather than merely to accept them. They are taught to weigh statements and arguments, and to come to their own conclusions, which may be different from those of their teachers. This is because, in many ways, modern educational systems are based on what we call Cartesian philosophy. It was the French philosopher Descartes who, in the seventeenth century, laid the foundations of what we call Rationalism. In general, he concluded that we must doubt everything until we can prove it to be true. Moreover, the proof required is what is known as empirical proof, derived from what we can see and feel, measure and weigh. So it appears to be a healthy thing for our children to challenge statements and ideas, and to ask for proof.

When I was a minister of a church, I frequently came across bewildered middle-aged parents whose children were for ever asking 'Why?' They would tell their children to do this or not to do that, only to be met with 'Why?' Pity the poor parent who could only reply, 'Because it's the done thing', because that kind of answer also invites the question, 'Why?'! I had a good deal of sympathy with both sides. The parents were trying to get across what they felt was right and proper, for that is what they had been taught themselves. The youngsters were simply doing what they had been taught to do, and that was to doubt and question everything until they could prove it to be valuable or relevant.

This, of course, has far-reaching effects when it comes to what we believe. If what the Bible says, for instance, is incapable of 'proof', people feel that they can discard it. As it is, it has become popular to be cynical, and to debunk everything. That includes not only religion, but also politics, and law, and education itself—in fact, anything they can get their hands on.

In practice, it means that agnosticism has become very fashionable. Ask about spiritual things—or about a good many of the important issues of life—and people will often reply, 'We can't really know, because we can't prove things one way or the other. I prefer to remain agnostic.' It sounds very discerning and mature to say 'I'm keeping an open mind on this or that'—rather like a dustbin with the lid off! It is certainly a very convenient way out of any real commitment to say that we cannot really know, and therefore we do not have to act.

Of course, there are many things that we will never know, but when this attitude becomes someone's whole philosophy of life, the results are pathetic. It leaves people with no clear guidance about the real business of living. It is morally and spiritually paralysing. But where do we go today for guidance and direction? We have been schooled in doubt.

Man without God

If man can cope by himself, and if he is getting better and better, then, in spite of his doubts, he has no real need of God. He certainly has no need for a God he cannot prove to his satisfaction in a laboratory. In fact, for many, belief in God is seen as a positive hindrance to progress. It was another philosopher, Nietzsche, who described modern man as 'man come of age'. What he meant was that man had outgrown God, so that he no longer had any need for God. He could live perfectly well without having to worship or pray to anything.

This is something of the meaning of the phrase 'God is dead'. It means that the term 'God' no longer has any significance for modern man. He is secular man, satisfied with the things of time and sense. To believe in God is obscurantist. It is head in the sand, a sort of throw-back from the past when our ignorance demanded that we had a God to run to. It is argued that we can now stand on our own two feet, and live perfectly well without the God-dimension in our lives at all. Hence religion is seen as childish.

Whether people have actually thought it through like this or not, in practical terms this is how many live. They are practical atheists. In spite of a variety of superstitious practices, they have no God, and they live as though he does not exist. This is another assumption running right through modern, Western society that we get thrown at us from every angle. The clever, worldly man can live without God; the religious man is a fool and an idiot.

What does the church say?

Even Christians who are committed to faith in God and Christ have been brought up and educated like the rest. They are children of their own time. Inevitably, the way in which the world thinks influences the way in which Christians think, unless we are very careful.

We see this in their own attitude to authority. For years, the Bible was regarded as God's word, and therefore as having something definitive to say about life and death, truth and error. In the last century this kind of confidence began to be eroded inside the church. We may broadly label the movement as 'Modernism', in that it was assumed that whatever did not fit in with current, modern thinking must be modified or discarded. Hence if I read something in the Bible that does not accord with the way in which people are thinking today, I am entitled either to ignore it or to reinterpret it. Modernists argue that Scripture can no longer be seen as the divinely inspired record of God's gracious intervention in human affairs. It must be regarded as just one more chapter in fallible man's long search for higher things. Israel becomes a race with particular religious genius. And Jesus Christ? He was a gifted and outstanding moral teacher and spiritual leader, to be bracketed with others like Buddha or Muhammad.

If this is so, how did the church get hold of the idea

that he was the Son of God? This, we are told, was never his intention. It was the misinterpretation of what he said and did—or what early Christians thought that he said and did—especially as his teaching got out into the Greek world where they were used to gods and goddesses. So, what we have understood as Christian orthodoxy for nearly 2,000 years was really an accident of history. But modern, enlightened man knows better, and he adjusts his beliefs accordingly.

One area where this thinking is all too obvious is the whole subject of miracles in the Bible. Living as we do in a world that demands proof in the form of weighing, measuring, seeing and the like, it is argued that there can be no such things as miracles. They cannot be repeated in laboratory experiments, and therefore they do not happen. It is as simple as that. Babies are not born from virgins nowadays, so you cannot believe in the virgin birth of Christ. People do not rise from the dead nowadays, so you cannot have a resurrection on the third day.

Either the writers of the Gospels got things wrong, or they sincerely misinterpreted events that have a perfectly rational explanation. Because of this, you can pick up many modern books about the Bible and find the miracles explained away as natural occurrences in one way or another. The belief in the supernatural that arose from them is accounted 'myth'.

This is a term that is used by many modern biblical scholars, but in a somewhat different sense from the usual one of 'fairy stories'. It is supposed to represent the particular approach that people in any generation have to the world in which they live. We have our myths in this way, just as they had their own in Bible times. The problem, it is claimed, is that they are different. The Bible authors obviously thought in terms of the supernatural, while we are secular people who have no need for the supernatural.

For all his sophistication, when you beat the modern scholar down to what he means by myth, it sounds very little different from what we usually understand by that word. Did the events described in the Gospels really happen? Did God's Son come into this world and live among us as a man? Did he die on the cross for our sins and rise again on the third day? Did he return to his Father, and will he be coming back one day? To the Modernist, the answer to questions like these must be, 'No, it could not actually be so, because of what we know nowadays.'

It appears, at first glance, that this kind of teaching would be welcomed by modern people, but it certainly has not been that way in practice. What started in the colleges, and spread to the pulpits and into the schools, has emptied the gospel of any real authority and power that it had. Men in the ministry, commissioned to preach and teach the word of God, are not sure what the word of God is. People in the pews, expecting a clear lead, are perplexed and discouraged. No wonder so many have stopped attending church altogether. There was nothing for them there.

Children receiving their compulsory religious education in schools fare little better. The teachers are sometimes so unsure themselves about what to believe or teach, that they can do no more than introduce their pupils to a vague mish-mash of religions, where one is as good as the other, and none can really command respect or obedience. Added to this, the average TV image of the Christian faith is either one of bumbling irrelevance or theological impotence. No wonder modern man has little time or place for God when those who are supposed to know about him often fail to give a definitive answer or a positive lead.

Unbelieving faith

There may be many reading this book who know better. As sincerely as they know how, they have tried not to get sucked into the system. By the grace of God, they have been led not only to a personal faith in Jesus Christ, but also to a confidence in God's word. It deeply disturbs them when they see the unbelief and ungodliness around them, and they are committed to a biblical gospel to the point where they are prepared to share what they know with a largely unresponsive world.

Yet even these believers might not be proof against the subtle influences of the wisdom of the world. Being children of our own time, it is possible for us to read the Bible while at the same time unconsciously distinguishing between what happened then and what can happen now. We are prepared to accept the miraculous in the life of Jesus or in the book of Acts, and yet we find it difficult to accept that God can do things like that nowadays. We pray, and ask God to bless our churches, but how often do we have a real expectancy that God will act? As a result, we tend to be content with a mediocre church life or personal experience, professing our faith, and worshipping the Lord, but not really believing that he is the same living God who can actually do miracles today.

When did you last have a miracle in your church? It seems to have been the daily run of things in the book of Acts. You may answer that when someone is converted it is a miracle. You are right, but how often does it happen? In those early days, they got used to the Lord adding to their number daily. If an outsider came into your fellowship, could he feel the life of God running through it? What have you to offer to the world that is different? What can we, as Christians by God's grace, do that they cannot do? For all our evangelical ortho-doxy, many of our churches are far removed from New Testament reality. For all our worship and prayer, some would actually prefer to keep God at a safe distance.

It is because of all this that, unconsciously, we begin to water down the implications of the gospel message, and in particular the claims of Christ on people's lives. We talk about discipleship with the unwritten rider that, as we live in the twentieth century, we are entitled to modify its demands. So mediocre church life is matched by mediocre Christian living. The salt loses its taste. The water gets into the boat. The church becomes conformed to the world in the way that it thinks.

Christian thinking

Is there any antidote to all this? On the surface of things, the problem seems quite hopeless. We are reared and educated into a secular view of reality. We are being perpetually conditioned by that understanding of things. How ever can we escape its influence?

We might start by having a look at the whole subject of knowing. We must acknowledge the blessings of both education and knowledge. There is nothing in Scripture that tells me that, on conversion, I must commit intellectual suicide. On the contrary, when I commit myself to Christ, my mind becomes very important. When Paul tells us that we must not be conformed to this world, he also says that we must be transformed by the renewal of our *minds* (Rom 12:2). The term he uses here is taken straight from the Greek way of seeing things. They placed great emphasis on the mind and on thinking. They were among the world's first real philosophers. The apostle agrees with them that the mind is important, and that the way we think is crucial.

Or take, for example, his prayer for the Colossian church. He asks God that they might 'be filled with the knowledge of his will in all spiritual wisdom and understanding' (Col 1:9). From the beginning, teaching formed an essential part of church life (Acts 2:42). If the New Testament letters were abbreviated sermons, what must the sermons have been like? The apostles were convinced that, if their friends were to grow as Christians, they had to think, and they had to learn.

It might be a good thing to remember that, at a purely secular level, it has been Christians who have pioneered the education system as we know it. This is not only true in Europe. There are many places in the world where the best education available is in schools with a Christian foundation. In fact, sometimes the only education available to ordinary people is that offered by Christian missionaries or teachers.

Unfortunately, because of the trends that we have been discussing, there have been Christians who have reacted strongly, not only against worldly wisdom, but also against any kind of intelligent approach to the Christian faith. That is why evangelical Christians are sometimes charged with being obscurantist, and with refusing to face the facts.

I am always a little surprised at the criticism we receive from some quarters in the theological college where I work. We are unashamedly committed to the authority of the Bible as the word of God, and our aim is to train men and women to handle it honestly and spiritually. However, because we ask them to think through their faith, and to ask themselves questions about its validity, we are sometimes charged by those who we thought were our friends with Modernism. Unfortunately some of the arguments which are sometimes used do not reveal spiritual insight at all, but rather an ignorance of the issues involved.

When you look at the history of the church, the most effective apologists and defenders of the faith have been, and still are, those who have dedicated their intellect to the cause of Christ. For example, many a modern seeker has been indebted to an author like C. S. Lewis, who had a thorough grasp of Christian principles, and yet was able to combine it with a deceptively simple style. Many a person with intellectual difficulties born out of the worldly atmosphere in which we have to live has come to faith in Christ and the gospel through his work.

Maybe your problems are not deeply intellectual. Maybe for you it is a matter of knowing what to believe in a confusing and misleading world. What I have just been saying is just as true at the simpler levels of life. The only antidote to the insidious poison of worldly wisdom is not to think less, but to think more. What we need to do is to so fill our minds with God's word that we actually begin to think his thoughts.

How often have you been stumped by some doorstep heretic who has come along, and said, 'Here you are. It says this in the Bible'? You may have instinctively felt that what he was saying was wrong, but you did not know enough about your faith to be able to answer him. Or the fellow at work who is always asking those awkward questions about the Bible? How do you cope with him?

We really have no excuse. We not only have the Bible in numerous modern translations, we also have many effective tools that help us to study and understand it, especially in English. Christians whose mother tongue is different from ours often say how much they envy English-speaking believers. Most of the world's major Bible teaching aids are in English and are at our disposal. We have all we need when it comes to thinking through our faith in a secular and atheistic world.

What can we know?

As Christians, however, we must go deeper than this. We must ask about the world's presuppositions, that is, about its starting point and what it assumes in this whole business of thinking and knowing. We must question some of the modern myths that are swallowed whole by so many people.

Take this matter of how we know things. Is it true that we can only really know the things we can prove, by seeing, measuring, weighing and the like? Is it correct to say that everything must be explained in terms of cause and effect? Strange to say, there is even one branch of science that has opened up this question in the study of what is called parapsychology. It has faced up to the whole range of human experience that has always proved to be somewhat embarrassing in a strictly cause-and-effect world. It deals with things like ESP, telepathy, precognition, and the like, all aspects of human experience that have been long exploited by the world of the occult, but which are far more common than many in the past would admit.

Take, for example, the very common experience of knowing something before it happens, which we call precognition. Ask any group of people, and you will be surprised that most will admit that they have had odd occasions when this has happened to them in one way or another. Whereas some experiences may be explained away as pure coincidence, that does not account for all the occurrences. However, this drastically alters our understanding of what knowing is all about. As far as the 'proof' approach to events is concerned, it ought to take place afterwards. The happening is the cause, our knowledge is the effect that follows. Precognition, knowing something *before* it happens, reverses the whole order. One of the reasons why many a biblical scholar has rejected prophetic prediction in the past is that, according to them, you cannot know something before it happens. We are only just beginning to face up to the fact that you can, even though it stands many of our assumptions on their heads.

What price secular optimism?

What about this matter of moral and spiritual progress? We only have to read a little history to learn that civilizations do progress, but that they also regress; that peoples who have known peaks of intellectual and cultural achievement can also plunge into darkness, and even be forgotten entirely for years. The rosy, optimistic view of man as his own saviour certainly has little to support it from the events of the last few years. We still live in a world where life can be incredibly cheap, and where man can be insanely self-destructive. Man's inhumanity to man has not really decreased as the years have gone by. We merely sin in more advanced and sophisticated ways.

Is modern man as grown up and independent as he thinks he is? Are we able to cope without God and the traditional values that went into the making of Western society? It is very significant that the old optimism is waning somewhat, and a new mood is setting in that is just the opposite. Some of the very same scientists and philosophers who have professed to give us a lead in the past, are now admitting that things are getting out of control. Instead of moving inevitably towards our Utopia, we are told that we are well on the way to wiping ourselves out completely. It could be nuclear war, or over-population or starvation; it could be disease; it could be several other things that might tip the delicate balance of conditions necessary for life on our planet, and finish us off once and for all.

Groping in the dark

Over against the self-assertive confidence of worldly optimism, we have seen another trend in modern thinking. A secular view of life, which reduces man to being merely another animal, fails to satisfy a deep longing in the human heart. Instinctively man knows that he is more than just another thing.

This is why the philosophy called existentialism has been so very popular in recent years. Man needs something that will give his existence meaning and significance. He needs purpose in life. He needs to know who he is and where he is going, and secular materialism cannot supply that.

There have been numerous suggestions as to how he might find the answer, most of them centring on experience of some sort or another. It is this that contributes to the modern preoccupation with sex, and the modern abuse of drugs. A good deal of violence may be motivated by a feeling of being trapped in a meaningless existence. Much of the pop subculture illustrates the way in which these feelings are being exploited among young people who, to those not in on the scene, appear to be irresponsible in the extreme. Perhaps we might understand them better if we see them as a generation looking for something they cannot find. It is this, among other things, that makes young people wide open to authentic experience of Christ and his power in their lives.

After all, is it right to say that modern man is less religious than his forebears? In the sense that he has abandoned the traditional forms of religion, this would be so, but there are plenty of indications that he still feels the need of a dimension other than the purely secular. He has certainly not grown out of his superstitions. It seems rather pathetic to hear people in responsible positions admitting that they think some things bring them luck.

At the other extreme, interest in the supernatural is certainly not dead. The spiritual vacuum left when we were taught to discard biblical faith and experience has been filled with a growing obsession with the darker side of the spiritual world. It is striking that, after rearing two or three generations in secularism, we are seeing a current upsurge in occultism, satanism, black magic, witchcraft and the rest. One only has to review some of the more successful films, run one's eye over the magazines in the local newsagent, or look the subject up at the local library to see that, even if God is supposedly dead, Satan appears to be alive and well.

The real need

In fashion or out of fashion, the Bible has told us over the years that we cannot save ourselves. Man's need is not education, good as that may be, nor is it clever-sounding Humanism. Man is in moral and spiritual bondage. He needs redemption. He not only needs a pattern for living, he needs the wherewithal to live it out. Christians themselves need to be convinced that there is no other possible way out. We need to admit that, in the past, the church has not always been faithful in its diagnosis of human need, and opted for something less than the biblical gospel.

Back in 1880, when the view of the future was much more rosy than it is now, someone wrote a hymn that went like this:

> These things shall be: a loftier race
> Than e'er the world hath known shall rise,
> With flame of freedom in their souls,
> And light of knowledge in their eyes.

It goes on in that vein for six verses, reciting man's gentle dominion over the earth, his peaceful coexistence with his fellows, his noble pursuit of the arts, and so on. I may be misinterpreting the writer of the hymn, but if he was referring to this world this side of the second coming of Christ, he was both misled and misleading. Even in the hundred years or so since it was written, we have had a chance to embark on the grand experiment. We have reared several generations in educational systems that have been progressively refined to produce that end. It is highly questionable whether we have improved the situation at all. People know more but, as

Shaftesbury said years ago, when you educate people without giving them moral principles to live by, all you produce are clever devils! You cannot change fallen human nature by any educational process, by social reform, by Act of Parliament or by anything else human. Man is lost. He cannot save himself. God has to step in.

The real truth of the matter is that man is not for ever reaching after what is higher and better. He is certainly not continually seeking after God. Mostly, he is running away from him, or coldly indifferent to his claims. That is why God had to break into human history in order to make himself known. The Bible is the record, not of man seeking God, but of God seeking man. He did it in a variety of ways but, of course, pre-eminently in Jesus Christ. He sought us in a way that undermines our pride and self-sufficiency: he sent his Son to die on a cross in our place.

This is what Paul meant when he told the Corinthian Christians that the preaching of the cross was folly to the lost (1 Cor 1:18). For the cross refuses to be fitted into any neat, human philosophical system. It contradicts human expectations, because it passes judgement on man and his cleverness. It tells us of our basic inadequacy and need, that we are sinners and lost. The cross says that Christ had to die for you. In New Testament terms, the way of salvation is not the way of worldly cleverness, but the way of broken admission of failure. Even the cleverest have to come to the point of admitting that, if they are going to prove what only God can do for man.

Knowing and living

The Bible authors would have found our modern educational system deficient at another point as well, for a number of our educational assumptions are not biblical at all, but classical Greek. The Greeks, as Paul discovered when he visited Athens, loved to hear and to share any new thing that came their way (Acts 17:21). They sought knowledge for its own sake. To gain knowledge was an education. The Bible authors were considerably more practical. They were certainly concerned about knowing, but it was always with doing in view. Paul's prayer for his Colossian friends that we cited earlier is not just a prayer for knowledge. The spiritual wisdom and insight that he prays for them must lead on to a life 'worthy of the Lord, fully pleasing to him, bearing fruit in every good work' (Col 1:10). That sums up the biblical attitude perfectly. Knowledge always involves responsibility.

When students come to our Bible College, I generally warn them that they will be considerably more answerable on the judgement day at the end of the course than they are at the beginning. It is good to accumulate knowledge, as long as we remember that, one day, God is going to ask us what we have *done* with it.

Herein lies the weakness of theological education. It could be half baked if we are not careful. We have made a great deal of teaching and educating. We have put our prospective ministers and missionaries through theological courses, and awarded them degrees and diplomas if they have been academically successful. We sometimes forget that, in and of themselves, these things are just paper. Consequently, the preaching and teaching in our churches can remain at a somewhat theoretical level. People hear the words, and know the facts, but are often very slow to translate them into solid practice. They become content with a cerebral Christianity that does not touch their lives.

In New Testament times, the proof of the gospel message was that it worked. It changed the whole life-style of those who accepted it. It was not merely an alternative theory or philosophy. It was what we call today a dialectical message that addressed real human needs, and offered an answer to them. People did not become Christians because of the clever arguments of the preachers. As Paul had to point out to those pseudo-intellectuals, the Corinthians, he preached a simple message in the power of the Spirit, and they had been converted (1 Cor 2:1–5). Those who responded to it proved its truth in their daily lives. For the message of the gospel is not just additional information. It carries with it a dynamic that revolutionizes even ordinary lives, and makes them extraordinary.

The weakness of so much contemporary idealism is not that it is unworthy. It is that it is all too often naïve. It assumes that, given what is right and honourable, men and women will rise to it. Unfortunately, as we shall see, human nature is so bent that sometimes what is right and honourable merely provokes further rebellion. We need more than good and high ideals. We need the power to put them into practice, and this is what becomes available to the simplest believers when they put their lives at Christ's disposal. Arguments or no, they just know that the gospel is true because they are experiencing its power daily in their lives.

Do you remember the man born blind whom Jesus healed (Jn 9:1–41)? When called before the council, who were convinced that it could not have happened that way, he had only one thing to say: 'One thing I know, that though I was once blind, now I see.' A similar enlightenment takes place whenever someone comes to a real encounter with Christ. It does not come by education or theorizing or philosophizing. God, by his Holy Spirit, takes the initiative in our experience as he had to in history. Then we know the gospel to be true, whatever our previous opinions, and we go on to prove progressively that it is true in daily experience.

I was once told that a man with a theory is always at the mercy of a man with experience, and I have proved that to be so. In the face of the world's cleverness in all its subtle, God-denying forms, we can only say that the old-fashioned, unsophisticated gospel is both true and powerful. It does for us what no theory or philosophy could ever do, in that it deals with our real need. It is God's answer to man's sinfulness, which means that, at last, we have ideals that are liveable. Consequently, when we are faced with the high-flown intellectualism of a world that thinks it knows better, we prefer the word of God.

4. Right and Wrong

There is nothing that a sailor likes less than fog. In a very short time, what appears to be a clear, bright day can contract to a little circle around the boat blocked in on all sides by a dense white wall. There is nothing to see. Even sound plays strange tricks, and it is very easy to lose yourself, and to sail well off course, or even in circles. In a similar way, we are living in a generation that has lost its moral bearings. Whereas in the past most would have some idea of 'right' and 'wrong', the situation is now so confused that the average person is at a loss to know where to go for his or her standards. They are living in a moral fog, and the church, which ought to lead the way, is either not listened to, or is so ambiguous in its statements that it has little impact on society at large. No wonder many a Christian finds himself facing a dilemma when deciding what he ought or ought not to be doing.

Pick up any newspaper and you will not be able to read very far without coming up against moral values that are anything but Christian. In church we may be taught about justice, truth, love, loyalty, unselfishness and the like. Out in the world, these virtues are fast being abandoned at every level of society. Whereas

Britain might have been known once as a 'Christian country', in that, by and large, the standards of Christian morality were officially accepted, it certainly could not be called that today. Both individually and corporately we are in a moral mess. Those who were brought up with the old values and standards are bewildered in a society where, it seems, almost anything goes, while young people, who have never known anything else, grope their way by trial and error learning the hard way, if at all.

Who's to say?

As we have said, this crisis in morality is largely the result of a crisis in authority. In the days when people believed that God had revealed what he wanted to mankind, that authority was in place and unquestioned. Right and wrong were related to a holy God, who loved justice, truth and mercy. But God's authority, along with all other authority, has been open to question for some years now, and even within the churches. However, if you discard God, the absolute standard, everything becomes relative. As the Russian novelist Dostoevsky once said, where there is no God, all things are allowable. What he meant was that when you have knocked God out of the way in which you think, you have no absolute moral authority, because you have no absolute truth. In practice it means that we can be absolutely sure of nothing. We have nothing outside ourselves to which we can turn for that assurance. If there is no God to tell us what to do, who can? It means that every man's opinion has equal value. What might be right for one could equally be wrong for another, for no one can say any more, 'This is right' or 'This is wrong'. People are generally left to make up their own minds.

This approach not only challenges what we have traditionally regarded as spiritual truth, the truth that God has revealed about himself, but it also questions the accumulated moral experience of society. Over many years of living together, people come to a collective wisdom about what is good for them, but this now equally comes under scrutiny and judgement. Tradition and custom are dirty words. They must be questioned and, if necessary, discarded. Why do this or that? Why be moral? What is morality anyway?

When we try to bridge the gap between the old and the young, we need to remember that, morally speaking, they have been brought up in different worlds. The way in which people think has changed, as we have seen, and therefore so has their whole attitude to life in general. The sad thing, of course, is that young people do not have the practical experience that they are so easily discarding. Too many—in their lives, their relationships and their marriages—are having to learn the hard way what many a generation has learned before them, not to say what the Bible says about these things.

The Humanist, who argues that we ought to be good and live for the sake of others without any religious authority or sanction, is very badly off. He is really asking for Christian ethics without the Christian gospel. If there is no God against whom we can measure our lives, why should anyone be kind, decent, just, honest, or work hard at any of the other virtues? Christian morality is a reflection of God's character. Dispense with God and, logically, you dispense with that kind of morality.

Actually, in biblical terms, you dispense with man

himself. After all, according to the Bible, man was made in God's image. He was made to reflect God in his character. But if there is no God, there is nothing to reflect. Man is reduced to either a complicated electro-chemical process, or to just another animal. If that is so, any kind of morality is logically a nonsense. You cannot expect a machine to know the difference between right and wrong. My car has no sense of morality. If I am reduced to a process, I am no better than that myself. Or again, if men and women behave like animals, we should not really be surprised—if, that is, we are only animals.

It is curious that few atheists would run to this extreme in their logic. One of the great universals in the world is some kind of morality. It may differ from place to place, and from group to group, but eventually every society, clan or organization ends up with some sort of moral code. We even speak about 'honour among thieves', because criminals have a fairly strict standard of what is and what is not acceptable among themselves. It is even more ironic that, in these days when we have discarded God and an absolute standard, we hear more about the 'rights' of individuals and groups than ever before. If atheistic men were logical, they would see that we have no 'rights' at all.

Everybody's doing it

In place of God's standards, we usually fall back on a sort of ethics of consensus. If everybody does it—or if it is socially acceptable—it must be right. Many a parent has battled with his or her growing children on those terms, when they have brought home an alien morality. 'But everybody's doing it . . .' is a fairly standard answer to pleas for traditional values.

Parliament, of course, reflects the trend, because we live in a democracy. Although there are certain patterns of behaviour that no government can really afford to allow, our elected representatives are not necessarily better equipped to make moral decisions than we are. They are the product of the same generation, and they also have an eye to their own popularity. So the laws that are passed become equally the result of an 'everybody's doing it' approach to morality.

In a democracy, if the law-makers as well as the governed are influenced by the same relative values, there is no defence against moral landslide. However, even if Parliament did require Christian standards of behaviour by law, it would be extremely difficult to enforce them if everyone disregarded them. You need a dictatorship to do that kind of thing. As it is, we have seen a progression of Bills go through Parliament which, from a Christian point of view, have legalized sin. The current legislation on abortion and homosexuality are just two examples. It was only because public moral standards had fallen well below Christian requirements that Bills like these could ever be brought to Parliament, let alone become the law of the land.

But law, in God's purpose, should serve as a restraint on the evil of human nature. This is why the New Testament writers could speak highly of even pagan magistrates (see, for example, Rom 13:1–7). Their job was to check the wicked and to encourage the good, and in that they were, unwittingly, God's servants. When the law is weakened, however, human nature begins to come out into the open. This is what Paul meant when he spoke about 'the works of the flesh' being 'fornication, impurity, licentiousness, idolatry, sorcery, enmity, strife, jealousy, anger, selfishness, dissension, party spirit, envy, drunkenness, carousing and the like' (Gal 5:19–21). In the final analysis it means 'Live for yourself and blow the rest.'

This is why we are living in such an irresponsible age. Duty is an old-fashioned word now discarded. Passing the buck is much more popular. The average person seems to want to get as much for himself for as little effort as possible, which is why the 'Protestant work ethic', which taught an honest day's work for a fair day's pay, is also out of fashion. Selfishness has become the order of the day at work, in the home, in relationships, within the family. Right and wrong are measured by 'what does me good' and what does not. When a situation becomes a bit uncomfortable, we feel free to chuck it in, whatever our original commitment. People look at marriage that way. Others conduct their businesses with the same philosophy. We are living through a time very much like the period of the Judges in the Old Testament when there was also a crisis of authority. 'There was no king in Israel; every man did what was right in his own eyes' (Judg 21:25).

Are we any better?

Have Christians got anything to say or to offer in this situation? Unfortunately, the world has got into the church to an alarming extent in terms of simple morality, so that the outsider can often justly point the finger and tell us, 'You're no better'. It always makes a good newspaper story when the vicar runs off with the organist's wife, or when the church treasurer is caught with his fingers in the till. Whereas these may be the sensational exceptions rather than the rule, any minister will tell you that the average Christian often has real difficulty in maintaining Christian standards.

Unfortunately, whenever a group makes high moral claims—as Christians do—they are always open to the accusation, as well as to the sin, of hypocrisy. This has been true of the church in the past, and it can be so today. We can still have the Christian businessman who regularly attends church every Sunday, only to be engaged in shady dealings during the week. We can still find the Christian worker who teaches in the Sunday school but who fiddles his time-sheet. We can still come across the married person who is engaged in church activities, but who is less than faithful to his or her partner. What we do on Sundays and what we do through the week can be strangely divorced, until we too deserve the scorching criticism that Jesus levelled against the Pharisees.

Maybe this is why the good, old-fashioned teaching about holiness and love, or about the exclusive claims of the Lord Christ, are less popular in our churches than they once were. Maybe this is why conventions 'for the deepening of spiritual life' are seen as just a bit old-fashioned. The kind of challenge these things present is far too disturbing for people who are living double lives.

It is even worse when we spiritualize our irresponsibility. Part of the current reaction away from the old-time 'legalism' is nothing more than this. To have actual rules to keep and guidelines to follow is deemed 'bondage', and unspiritual by some. We are told that we must feel led of the Lord when it comes to what we do or do not do. There are some who will not even commit themselves to a church fellowship because it would be 'unspiritual'. What it often means is that they do not want to get involved in anything that looks like hard work. That is one of the reasons why, in so many of our churches, it is the willing few who actually sustain the programme and get on with the jobs.

Perhaps it is most noticeable in our attitude to the outsider, the man or woman still without God and without hope in the world. There is a startling contrast between the way in which the first Christians spontaneously shared their faith with unbelievers and the laboriously organized 'efforts' in our present-day churches. The 'couldn't-care-less' attitude of the world has seeped into the church to the point where it no longer concerns some Christians that their neighbours, families and non-Christian friends are going to hell. They would be quite happy with Cain's response when asked about Abel, 'Am I my brother's keeper?' (Gen 4:9). Yet these are people who profess to know the love of God in Christ which brought him down to us, and which took him to the cross for us.

Maker's instructions

When God made that special agreement with his people that we call the Old Covenant or Testament, he imposed upon them certain standards that reflected his own character. They had a God who was holy, righteous, just, true, faithful, merciful and loving—and who expected people called by his name to be the same. For their sake, his requirements were enshrined in his written Law. They were told in no uncertain terms things like 'You shall not steal', 'You shall not kill', 'You shall not commit adultery'. There were many times in their history when they wandered far from him and his Law, and suffered for it. For Israel's God was not like some of the pagan deities of the surrounding countries, unconcerned with morality. It was an essential part of his relationship with them.

When God gave man his Law in this way, he was not joking. He was concerned for them and for their good. When we buy some new appliance for the home, if we are sensible, we read the maker's instructions. If we fail to run it within its limits, or if we neglect it, we should not be surprised if it does not last, or if it breaks down. By discarding God's Law, modern society has done just that. The moral chaos we see in the West today is because man thinks he knows better than God.

As Christians we need to be reminded that, when the gospel came along, God did not pension off his Law. Jesus pointed out that he had not come to abolish the Law, but to fulfil it, and he gave us a few striking examples of what this would mean. Murder was an attitude of the heart; adultery, similarly, was lust; love extended to those who hate us. This was the kind of morality he expected from his followers (Mt 5:17–48).

This kind of requirement is well beyond anything that we could ever achieve ourselves. In fact our human nature is such that God's Law is humanly unattainable. This is why the gospel not only offers forgiveness for past sins, but also power to succeed where otherwise we would fail miserably. This is the ministry of the Holy Spirit who lives within the believer, changing him or her progressively into the likeness of Christ himself. The results of his activity, what Paul calls 'the fruit of the Spirit', are 'love, joy, peace, patience, kindness, goodness, faithfulness, gentleness, self-control' (Gal 5:22–23). Against these, he adds, there is no law, for the simple reason that they are the fulfilling of the spirit of the Law. This is what God wants. He does for us and in us what we could never do for ourselves. 'The just requirement of the Law' can be 'fulfilled in us who walk, not according to the flesh', that is, our old human natures, 'but according to the Spirit' (Rom 8:3–4).

In practice, this means that if someone makes a profession of Christ, we may legitimately expect to see a change in their behaviour. They may need teaching and instructing as to what God wants them to do or not to do, but something has gone very wrong indeed if there is no change at all. It follows that any deeper experience of the Holy Spirit should also result in more Christ-like behaviour. If someone professes to be full of the Spirit, we may quite fairly ask what they are like to live with, or how it affects the quality of their daily work. All in all, if the gospel is what we say it is, it should produce in us a lifestyle that is head and shoulders above that of the world.

This is no cause for self-righteousness. It is not our doing. It is all of God and his grace. We are merely called upon to co-operate with him, and we have a big enough reason for so doing.

Jesus is Lord

The gospel is not in the nature of a business deal; it is more like a love affair. I may transact a business arrangement because I see the benefit of it in terms of a good offer or a favourable investment. When I fall in love, I fall in love. There is something about that other person that captivates me to the point where I willingly put my life at their disposal. God is not only offering us the most favourable terms on the market, he is offering us his love in Christ. The self-giving love of the Lord Jesus becomes the only adequate motive for the surrender of faith which is our response to the gospel. 'The love of Christ controls us', says Paul, quite literally, 'hems us in to a course of action' (2 Cor 5:14).

To speak about the Lordship of Christ apart from the love of Christ is to describe the worst kind of tyranny, for Christ demands everything from his followers. He tells them that, if they would come after him, it will involve self-denial, even death to self-interest. He must come first in everything and in every way. Those were the terms on which the earliest preachers called men and women to faith. Jesus must be Lord, and those who named him as such must therefore submit to his discipline and direction.

And they did it willingly, because of what they knew of his love. This is why the Christian cannot carelessly follow the world's example when it comes to behaviour. He does not belong to himself any more. Christ must be Lord at home and at work, within the family or among friends. Christ must be Lord of habits and thoughts, of actions and reactions. They answer the 'everybody's doing it' argument with 'but what does *he* want?' No sacrifice, no commitment, no effort, no discipline can ever be too great, in that he has already given himself for us. The opinion of the world is replaced by the approval of Christ.

All must answer

In this way, a truth well known in the Old Testament comes into even greater prominence. We live out our lives under God's gaze, and ultimately we all have to answer to him for what we are and do. This sense of accountability is what was known as 'the fear of God'. God's people were not just responsible to one another or to some civic authority. They were responsible to God for literally everything. The fact that they must answer to him one day restrained them from doing what they would otherwise regret. Conversely, when they fell into bad ways and disregarded his Law, it could be summed up in similar terms: 'There is no fear of God before their eyes' (Rom 3:18).

In the New Testament, this old truth is heightened by the fact that the one we call Lord and Saviour will return one day to be our Judge. 'We must all appear before the judgement seat of Christ, so that each one may receive good or evil, according to what he has done in the body' (2 Cor 5:10). Salvation is by faith. We take the gift of God so freely offered through his Son. But, as we have said, if our experience is the genuine thing, this will lead to a change of behaviour. That is why judgement is by works.

When Jesus told the parable of the Sheep and the Goats, the dividing line between the two classes was how each had lived. It will not be a matter then of what we have professed, if our profession has not been backed by lifestyle. It will carry no weight at all if we have not lived for Christ in our ordinary duties and commitments (Mt 25:31–46).

We see this principle beautifully illustrated in the advice Paul gave to Christians who were slaves (Col 3:22–25). They had no choice in what they did or did not do, and some had very hard masters. But the apostle told them to work hard and consistently, and not only when they were being watched. They should fear the Lord in that they should remember that he saw what they did even if no one else did. What is more, although they appeared to be working for an earthly master, Paul could tell them, 'You are serving the Lord Christ'. If first-century slavery could be turned into Christian service, so can your work at home, or in the office, school or factory. As you do that job for him, you too are serving the Lord Christ. I once heard of a typist who typed her letters as though the Lord Jesus was going to sign them rather than her boss. She had got hold of this truth.

We are repeatedly told in Scripture that Christian 'activities' are no replacement for this kind of Christian living. Too many opt out of their duties as partners or parents to get involved in 'church-work'. Too many are less than efficient in their daily employment, but over-active in religious affairs. Jesus warned us that 'on that day many will say to me, "Lord, Lord, did we not prophesy in your name, and cast out demons in your name, and do many mighty works in your name?" and then I will declare to them, "I never knew you; depart from me you evildoers"' (Mt 7:22–23).

Words like these may be very uncomfortable, and may disturb our complacency, but, like God's Law of Old Testament times, they are for our good. They tell us exactly where we stand in a world that says that morals do not matter. When the sailor is caught by fog, the rule to follow is to take bearings before it closes in, and then to work from that position even when 'sailing blind'. Nowadays we also have radio direction finders that help us to fix where we are even though we cannot see a thing. These God-given principles are like that.

However, on the occasions when I have been at sea and overtaken by fog, I have noticed a peculiar thing. Although I may have fixed my position, there is a great temptation to stop trusting my instruments. Although the compass tells me that I am going in the right direction, it does not 'feel' right. Although my radio direction finder is working perfectly, somehow the position it gives me does not look 'right' in the chart. And yet I ignore them at my peril, in the same way that I ignore God's word at my peril.

'Do not be deceived', wrote the apostle, 'God is not mocked, for whatever a man sows, that will he also reap' (Gal 6:7). You cannot play fast and loose with God's Law and get away with it. What God has entrusted to you he will one day require from your hand, and the Lord Jesus, whom you profess as your Saviour, will be himself your judge.

For Christian living is life with the roof off. It is not simply a matter of putting up a respectable front to our neighbours and friends. It is being open to God, allowing him to direct and check our motives and attitudes and ambitions. What I do and why I do it must be pleasing to him, because the day is coming when both my actions and my motives will be open and revealed. The fear of the Lord may not be as high a motive for good living as love for the Lord, but sometimes when faced with the allure of the world and its practices, it is what we need.

5. Where Has Love Gone?

One of the most obvious expressions of the world's attitude to morality is what has come to be known as sexual permissiveness. In order to help us to get those bearings of ours, it might be useful to ask ourselves how the current situation has come about.

Sexual revolution

The present position is the result of a massive change in attitudes over the past thirty years or so. The general opinion today is that it really does not matter what consenting adults do together, and some would go even further to include young people and children. We have got used to the description of such behaviour as 'private morality', and successive governments have openly disclaimed responsibility for that area of life. According to our law-makers, the individual's sex life is his or her private affair. As a result, it is now widely accepted that anything goes in the area of sexual behaviour.

What has suffered most in this trend has been the traditional Christian attitude to marriage and, along with that, to extra-marital relationships and to homosexuality. I say 'traditional', because although Britain is no more or less essentially 'Christian' than it ever was, thirty years ago the traditional values were still around. Divorce was the exception rather than the rule. It still carried a certain amount of social stigma. The whole subject of sex was somewhat sacrosanct and, as a result, there were fairly tight controls on the way in which the subject was handled in the media.

These values are openly questioned nowadays, and in varying degrees have been discarded by the mass of people. It is always dangerous to generalize, but it is apparent that all sections of our society have been affected in some degree by this state of affairs, some radically.

Why has this happened? Why this enormous swing in such a short time? From a social point of view, this shift in sexual morality can be partly explained as a reaction away from the rigid approach of the last century and the early years of this one. 'Victorian' morality has not got a very good image these days. On the one hand it represents a stiff code of outward respectability combined with a refusal to admit—openly at least—that sex was an aspect of normal, healthy human life. On the other, it is argued, it bred a self-righteous hypocrisy in that it produced a double standard. Outwardly all was prim and proper; underground, though, all kinds of things went on. What is more, the whole approach was undergirded by an official religion that was equally stifling and repressive.

In the first half of this century, however, we have seen both a weakening of religious sanctions and the demoralization of two world wars. As well as shattering faith, war always destabilizes morality. But there has also been another factor that has contributed to the present situation. Psychologists, drawing heavily on the work and theories of Freud, have argued that sexual repression is the root of all kinds of personality malformation. Some argue that not only does the silent approach to sex generate fear, ignorance and frustration, but that it is positively harmful to our whole mental balance. For some psychologists, the cause of most of man's problems is the mishandling of sex and, as the Christian faith has traditionally applied restraints and sanctions in this area, Christianity is attacked because of this.

I think that most would agree that there were many things in the old 'under the carpet' attitude to sex that were not only harmful, but actually unbiblical, and that sexual repression has caused a great deal of suffering. However, it is quite another thing to swing to the opposite extreme, and abandon restraint altogether. Human nature will run downhill as soon as you allow it to, especially when what it wants is given a semblance of legality.

Sex and the media

The whole process of change in this area has been accelerated by the development of the mass media, especially the visual media. What we are witnessing today is the exploitation of sex in advertising and entertainment, so that what was once a closed subject is now blasted at us wherever we go. You cannot ride on public transport without being barraged by posters that exploit sex. You cannot watch many programmes on TV without coming up against it in some form or another. You have to hunt hard to find a film showing that is not immoral. It is difficult to buy a paperback or a

magazine that does not confront you with the subject in
more or less explicit ways.

What concerns Christians should not be that the
subject has become open, but that in the process it has
become commonplace and cheap. More than this, it has
become obsessional in the generation in which we
have to live. You do not have to talk with non-Christians
for long without the subject coming up in some form or
another. What were innocent words and phrases have
taken on all kinds of double meanings. Society has
become sex-mad.

As with the other aspects that we have been con-
sidering, the conditioning to which we have been subjected has not always been brazen. It is often subtle and
low-key, but just as pagan in its effects. We see this in
the area of the modern novel or play. There, sex is
frequently regarded as not having any moral value at
all. It is simply assumed that it is something to be used
and enjoyed without any moral considerations what-
soever. People go to bed with one another. Marriages
break up. Divorce is commonplace. It is argued that
this is realism and life, but in reality it is part of a
chicken and egg situation. It is certainly because public
morality has eroded that these things happen, but one
of the most potent forces in that process has been this
subtle conditioning by the media. The control of the
media is in the hands of a fairly small group of opinion-
formers who have a great deal to answer for.

The same could be said for those newspapers that
print every lurid detail of the latest sex scandal because
it is 'news', or even under the pretence of exposing
corruption. In fact, editors have a very clear idea of
what appeals to fallen human nature, and what will
therefore sell their papers. But under the guise of

informing, they are actually conditioning people to
think in a certain way. What is shocking when first
proposed becomes accepted in five years simply because
people have been conditioned to accept it, by which
time the process has moved on to the next degree of
immorality.

Immorality and society

Although we are living under the particular pressures
of modern media techniques that have accelerated the
rate of change enormously, the process of demoralization is not new. History teaches us that, when a nation
goes into decline and becomes senile, it is almost always
accompanied by a breakdown in sexual morality. The
apostle Paul had to conduct his ministry in the ruins of
Greek culture. That is why, in the New Testament, we
discover the sort of conditions reflected that we see in
our own society today.

The Greeks had come to regard sex as simply another
appetite to be satisfied. If you were hungry, you had
something to eat. If you were thirsty, you got yourself a
drink. If you felt a sexual urge, you simply went and
satisfied it. That was their philosophy of life, by and
large, a philosophy that has emerged again in our own
society today.

But society cannot tolerate this kind of thing for long.
The great Roman empire, which superseded that of the
Greeks, fell in on itself for similar reasons. Morality of
all kinds became dispensable, and it ultimately
collapsed because it was rotten inside. History tells us
repeatedly that no strong nation can afford moral laxity
in this respect it is very interesting to see what
happened in Russia. In the early days after the Revolu-

tion, life was permissive, and it was the easiest thing in the world to get a divorce. Nowadays, it is much more difficult, for the simple reason that our communist friends learned the hard way that they could not build a strong society on the foundations of permissiveness.

Why this is so is really very simple. When sex becomes cheap, you undermine the basic building block of society, that is, home and family life. Society is made up of family units and, when they go, everything goes with them. That is the risk we run in the West; not just that venereal disease has reached epidemic proportions, or that legalized abortion keeps people needing surgery waiting for hospital beds, but that society is falling apart at the seams.

When I began my ministry about twenty-five years ago, we had to deal with marital breakdown, but it was the exception rather than the rule, even in the downtown area of London where our first church was situated. When we moved after a few years to a respectable suburb, we were surprised to come across far more. Now that we are working in the salubrious outer ring, we find that it is commonplace. We are repeatedly coming across people whose marriages are on the rocks, or who are separated from their partners, or who are suing for divorce.

What is even more concerning is the effect that all this has on the children, the kids who so often become almost unwanted pawns in the marital battle. What astonishes me is that we realize now better than we ever did what marriage break-up means to the children, and yet we have an utterly irresponsible attitude to marriage itself. Children need a secure, stable and loving home. Deny them this, and in some respects you scar them for life. The current epidemic of divorce can only result in a generation of psychological cripples.

We are concerned about delinquency in our schools, on our streets and in our football grounds. Very few appear to have the courage to say that this often derives from the moral chaos at home, and to raise their voices against popular opinion which says that, in the area of sex, anything goes. In the theological college where I live and work, we have some fine young Christians whose lives are still tormented by fears and depressions at times directly attributable to unstable home backgrounds. Part of my pastoral ministry is to help them through the psychological hang-ups that their parents have bequeathed to them.

This is why I object to the description 'private morality'. If this kind of behaviour so deeply and widely affects our society, it is not private at all. It is very much public morality. The damage is public and far-reaching. From a purely human point of view, spiritual considerations apart, there are very sound reasons why people ought to be concerned with what is going on around them. No nation can afford to allow what is happening in our nation today. Unfortunately we have politicians who are more concerned about power or vote-catching than they are about the public good, and who shuffle off their responsibility with a neat phrase like 'private morality'.

Under judgement

Christians, however, are not simply concerned from a historical or social point of view. From Scripture they have a spiritual assessment of what is going on. The decline in moral standards has gone hand in hand with a decline in vital spirituality. If you want an almost word-by-word description of our society, you must read the second half of the first chapter of Romans. What Paul says about pagan society in his day easily and readily applies to ours.

It begins with men and women refusing the truth that God has given them by turning away from him, and thus preferring to live a lie (vv. 18–23). In those days it was idolatry, but today men and women worship and serve 'the creature rather than the Creator' just as effectively. What does God do to a society like that? We are told three times that he gives them up (vv. 24, 26, 28)!

Although God's judgement will fully and finally fall on men and women on the last day, the Bible teaches that he also deals with sinful people here and now. One of the ways in which he does this is to lift the restraints he graciously lays upon us. We often complain about the amount of evil that God allows in the world. We would be surprised to learn how much he restrains. But when people deliberately and wilfully turn their backs on him, he lets them go their own way. It is almost as though he were saying, 'If you won't learn the easy way, learn the hard way', and he lets them go, headlong, down the path they have chosen for themselves.

Paul tells us that, although this results in all kinds of moral perversion (vv. 28–31), sexual immorality is an obvious expression:

> God gave them up in the lusts of their hearts to impurity, to the dishonouring of their bodies among themselves (v.24).

> God gave them up to dishonourable passions. Their women exchanged natural relations for unnatural, and the men likewise gave up natural relations with women, and were consumed with passion for one another, men committing shameless acts with men (vv. 26–27).

For when you lift the restraint on normal sexual relationships, it not only produces moral chaos, it also leads to sexual perversion. It is not at all surprising, therefore, that homosexuality is also hitting the headlines nowadays.

As we have seen, the current practical atheism has also devalued man. Instead of having dignity and value, he is reduced to a machine or an animal. This is seen nowhere better than in the matter of sex. The idea of a personal relationship with someone else is lost. Your partner becomes just a thing to be used and discarded, like a disposable tissue. In the end, sex itelf loses real significance beyond a means to momentary pleasure.

The world has welcomed modern permissiveness. It not only practises it; it applauds those who push on forward down the slippery slope. It calls moral licence 'freedom', ignoring the fact that lust can be a cruel and demanding master, and that sexual promiscuity can be slavery (2 Pet 2:19). It describes the pervert as 'gay', and sexual adventures as 'fun', but the New Testament calls a spade a spade. 'Be sure of this', wrote Paul, 'that no immoral or impure man, or one who is covetous [that is, an idolater], has any inheritance in the kingdom of Christ and of God. Let no one deceive you with empty words, for it is because of these things that the wrath of God comes upon the sons of disobedience' (Eph 5:5–6). You do not make sin less sin by giving it a pretty label. Nor do you avoid the judgement of God.

Living with it

If we are honest, we have to admit that everyone is feeling the pressure. We would not be human if we did not. We travel on the same trains and buses; we watch the same TV; we read the same newspapers. We are inevitably open to the same conditioning and, because of this, it is desperately easy for us to adopt worldly attitudes. In particular, we come to terms with the worldly acceptance of what is going on. We are told so often that everyone is doing it nowadays that we accept the state of affairs. We get to the point where we are no longer grieved or shocked.

Whatever we might say about Lot who went down to live in that proverbially permissive and perverted city of Sodom, we are told that it deeply distressed him. 'By what that righteous man saw and heard he was vexed in his righteous soul day after day with their lawless deeds' (2 Pet 2:7–8). In contrast, we find it all too easy to accept the standards and values, the sins and perversions of the world as the norm.

We can simply slip into it. I remember watching a TV programme once at a Christian friend's house. It was part of a well-produced serial, and after we had seen the episode through, he said, 'Let's watch the next programme. It's a comedian. He's good.' As I sat there looking in, I felt acutely embarrassed because every other joke was dirty or suggestive. When I ventured to comment on it later to someone else, I got the reply, 'Every comedian is like that nowadays.' It is in ways like this that Christians spend precious time watching shows in their living-rooms that they would never have dreamed of going out to a cinema to see. But we have lost our shockability. We say that this is the way things are, and therefore we must accept them as they are.

Taken in

In this whole game, young people are particularly vulnerable. From a very early age they are confronted with sex, and regularly in a most unhealthy format. I am not here opening the vexed question as to whether or not sex ought to be on the junior-school curriculum. There are arguments for and against, and a great deal depends on how it is taught whenever it is taught. My concern is that these things are thrown at children from every angle in their formative years until the permissive approach appears to be normal, ordinary and even healthy. Over against this, the biblical standards are portrayed as archaic and irrelevant.

This is true for the children of Christian as well as non-Christian homes. If we are not careful, our Christian young people learn more about love from the world than they do from the Bible. It sometimes means that, like the rest, they can go into married life with the wrong set of expectations, only to be disillusioned and frustrated. Like so many around them, they never understand the whole business of making and sustaining a personal relationship with someone else. Successful married life is assumed to be a successful sex life. What is more, they sometimes get sucked in as far as pre-marital sex is concerned, doing themselves untold psychological damage in the process. For we know that permissive young people find it extremely difficult to form a lasting, stable relationship, quite apart from the biblical teaching on the subject.

But all this is not only true for singles; married people are also feeling the pressure. It is a tragedy when any marriage breaks down, but it is a double, triple, tragedy when a Christian couple is involved. If you have ever had to deal with a situation like this, you will know how it hurts, and how far-reaching is the damage. On one occasion I learned that one of my own church officers, who was a young people's leader, had left his wife and children, and gone off with the girl from the office. As a pastor I felt as though I had been kicked; especially when I thought of the hurt and confusion among those who had loved and trusted him both in and out of his home and church.

It is even worse when a couple go into marriage with divorce as an option in mind if it does not work out. After all, that is the world's way of doing things. If we are not careful, we find ourselves, unconsciously at least, light-years from the biblical pattern of things.

Some of the blame for this kind of thinking must be laid at the door of the church itself. We have not taught about the Christian attitude to sex and marriage as clearly and as frankly as we should have done. In some quarters, it has been and is still a closed subject, in spite of the sexual revolution going on all around. Talking to a minister friend once about the need, and the possibility of running a course for youngsters in his church, I got the lame response, 'Oh, but I couldn't speak on that!'

Thank God that the Scriptures are more forthright than some Christian ministers. The Bible is quite straightforward on the subject of sex. For example, if you want a delightful description of intimate love between man and woman, read the Song of Solomon. I know that embarrassed Christians have long spiritual-ized it away into a picture of Christ's love for the church, but its real value is that it teaches something of the beauty and sanctity of sex and marriage. For this scripture is not only frank, it is reverent too. Compare

the Bible's handling of the subject with the crude and
explicit myths of paganism, and you will find that you
are in a different world. From the very beginning sex is
regarded, not as an opportunity for lewd description,
but as part of God's good creative design (Gen 1:27).
What is more, as with all his gifts, it involves both
privileges and responsibilities.

The place of sex

You cannot get away from the fact that, in the Bible, the
only proper place for sex is within the marriage relationship. It is the physical expression of a permanent
personal relationship between husband and wife. It
acts out in a very powerful way the mutual self-giving
of two persons to one another. It is part of a whole new
oneness that comes about when two people come
together in marriage, a oneness that finds right and
proper expression in children, a home, and shared life.

That is the biblical concept of marriage. It should be
the norm. Marriage break-up and divorce are not really
on the agenda at all. You come together for life.

If there are grounds for divorce in the New Testament,
they are those of adultery, which cuts across this exclusive relationship. But although realistic enough to
recognize the possibility, Scripture always presents the
ideal. Do you remember the time when Jesus was drawn
into debate with the Jews of his day about divorce
(Mt 19:3–9)? It was quite a divisive issue for them.
Those of the stricter school argued that the only
adequate ground for divorce was immorality, whereas
the more lax approach included all kinds of lesser, trivial
reasons. Jesus took them back to Genesis, and pointed
out that, when man and wife come together, they

become 'one flesh', that is, in biblical terms, one new social unit. What is more, God does the joining. It is almost as though he is taking them back to the Maker's instructions to show them how the thing ought to work. Then he added, 'whoever divorces his wife, except for unchastity, and marries another, commits adultery'.

If the place of sex is within marriage, it follows that any sexual relationship outside the marriage bond is a direct denial of this. I would even go as far as saying that what we call pre- or extra-marital sexual relations are a perversion in biblical terms, because they are a parody of what sex was designed to be. If that is so, all the other distortions of our sex instinct are most surely not only unnatural, but far from God's intention.

There is even a sense in which we might be able to say 'sex *is* marriage', for in the physical union the two become one. This was the ground for Paul's argument with the permissive Corinthians who saw no harm in spending the night with a prostitute (1 Cor 6:12–20). 'Do you not know that your bodies are members [literally 'limbs'] of Christ?' he asks. 'Shall I therefore take the members of Christ and make them members of a prostitute?' Then he cites the same verse from Genesis that Jesus did: 'the two shall become one'.

By that definition there is no such thing as pre-marital sex. In biblical terms, in God's sight, having sex with someone is marriage. That may create all kinds of problems with no easy answer, especially for the sexually permissive, but it is the way the Bible puts it. I have it on good authority that it was often this way in the Middle Ages too. Marriage then was not a civil contract; it was a matter of consent and consummation. When two people give themselves to each other in the act of sex, it is as much marriage in God's sight as marriage in a church or registry office.

I am not advocating 'private' marriage. We are living in a society where marriage is open, public and civil, and, in those terms, marriage between two Christians who pledge themselves to keep God's Law is a powerful witness. But let us remember the principle involved. In the Bible sex and marriage go together.

The difference Christ makes

The good news about Jesus Christ transforms everything that it touches. This is because it is not just a nice story or a noble philosophy. There is power in the gospel to change a life. On the one hand, we can have the assurance that the past is forgiven and blotted out; on the other, by the indwelling Spirit, we can look to God for grace to live a different kind of life. When Jesus forgave the adulterous woman, he also added, 'Go, and do not sin again' (Jn 8:1–11). In other words, he expected a change in the pattern of her behaviour. Forgiveness is not the easy, cheap thing that allows you to go off and commit the same sin again. Repentance involves breaking with the past, and making a new start.

There is a little phrase in one of Paul's letters that speaks volumes about the transforming power of the gospel. He tells the Corinthians once again, 'Do you not know that the unrighteous will not inherit the kingdom of God? Do not be deceived: neither the immoral, nor idolaters, nor adulterers, nor sexual perverts, nor thieves, nor the greedy, nor drunkards, nor revilers, nor robbers will inherit the kingdom of God. *And such were some of you*' (1 Cor 6:9–11). I find that fantastic. What Paul is saying is, 'Some of you were leading entirely immoral lives before you came to terms with the Lord Jesus Christ—and all that changed. Some of you were living in adultery—and it stopped. Some of you were homosexuals—and God gave you the power to overcome your unnatural lust.' These things belonged to the old life, and when they came in touch with the living power of Christ, they dropped away.

For Christ teaches us a new attitude both to ourselves and our own bodies, and to other people too. What is the dominant product of Christ living in us? It is *love*, the same word that has been so misused, prostituted and perverted. You begin to learn what real love is all about when you become a Christian. I always tell young people getting married that, if anyone should know how to love, Christians ought to. Paul teaches us that. He likens the love relationship of marriage to the love between Christ and his church, the love that took Jesus to the cross (Eph 5:21–32). As a standard for our loving that might dismay us, but we must remember that God can give us something of that quality of loving by the Holy Spirit who lives within.

When we preach the gospel we are not merely saying to permissive people, 'Look here. You've abandoned the old rules, but now you really must keep God's Law.' We are saying that Christ can come into people's lives in such a way that he can change their whole attitude to sex and relationships. As a Christian, you begin to value people as people. You do not regard them as merely things to be used any more. That is why the church ought to have a family atmosphere about it where we all feel a deep sense of belonging untainted by the lust that so often spoils relationships in the world.

What is true of Christian fellowship ought to be even more true of Christian homes. I believe that Christian homes where Christ is honoured and proved by husbands and wives, parents and children, are the most dynamic form of witness that we can present to the world today. We are demonstrating, in this way, how it really ought to be, and how Christ can give us the power to make it work. I also believe that, when couples get right with God, they can get right with one another; that Jesus Christ can revitalize marriages that are growing drab, and mend marriages that are broken.

The story is told of a couple whose marriage was on the rocks who, quite independently, found their way to one of Billy Graham's meetings. They both responded to the appeal at the end of the service, and came to know Christ personally. By one of those strange coincidences that the Lord often sets up, they saw each other across the counselling room, fell into one another's arms, and began again. God can do even that.

The part we play

But just as real and meaningful marriages do not simply 'happen', God's power does not operate automatically. We have to co-operate with him, if we are not only going to be proof against the world's conditioning in this area, but also if we are going to see God at work at this level. As Paul put it, God is at work in us, but we must work out our own salvation too (Phil 2:12–13).

We will never get on top of this subject until we know about personal discipline. It will affect what we do, what we read, where we look, what we see, and how we think. Jesus was speaking about personal discipline in the Sermon on the Mount when he used what, to our ears, is an extreme statement. In the setting of sexual temptation he says, 'If your right eye causes you to sin, pluck it out and throw it away' (Mt 5:29). This is what we call hyperbole. It was a way of highlighting the importance of something by putting it in an exaggerated way. I am sure that Jesus did not expect us to disfigure our bodies. The point is that, unless we discipline them, we will be led into sin.

Paul put it another way. He spoke about pummelling his body and subduing it (1 Cor 9:27). If you are not prepared to keep your body and its appetites in their proper place, you will open yourself wide to temptation. This means not doing certain things. For example, I read very widely, and have a great love for books of all kinds. But there are some authors whom I have sampled that I would not read any more. My old human nature is wicked enough without feeding it. Apply the same rule to the shows you watch, and the magazines you read, and the jokes you listen to, and anything else which you know represents a pagan view of sexual values. Job had this one sorted out years ago. When protesting his innocence to his friends, he could even say, 'I have made a covenant with my eyes; how then could I look upon a virgin?' (Job 31:1). He had made an agreement with himself that he would not look lustfully at the girls.

There is another extreme we need to be aware of at the same time. Whereas some of Paul's friends thought little of their misuse of sex, others adopted an almost inhuman attitude towards it. There were even husbands and wives who had stopped having sexual relations because they felt there must be something sinful about it. Paul makes it quite clear that they had got it all wrong. Whereas self-discipline is healthy, an unnatural denial of sex in marriage is both wrong and dangerous (1 Cor 7:1-7). As he points out, some may be able to live fulfilled lives without sex at all. For most of us, it is the most natural thing in the world to find satisfaction for the physical appetite God gave us in marriage.

Dealing with our sexuality is not just a matter of self-denial. There are positive principles involved too. When Paul was counselling the immoral Corinthians, he not only pointed out that their behaviour was completely inconsistent with their profession, he also reminded them that their bodies were 'temples of the Holy Spirit'; that they were not their own any more to do what they liked with; that they had been bought with a price. They were to glorify God in those bodies that they had once misused for merely physical self-gratification (1 Cor 6:19–20).

Elsewhere he puts it like this: 'Walk by the Spirit, and do not gratify the desires of the flesh' (Gal 5:16). That means that just as they were once driven by their physical urges and instincts, they could now be led by the inner prompting of the Holy Spirit. It would mean daily, hourly, listening for him and living by him. This only comes about as we yield heart and mind to him. It is then that we discover that God can actually lift us above the fog of worldly immorality, to live in his light and purity.

As always, it begins in the mind. The world may have conditioned our thinking, but so can the Spirit if we are prepared to co-operate with him. Paul points us away to the things that are honourable, just, pure, lovely, gracious, excellent and praiseworthy. 'Think about these things', he says (Phil 4:8). Sex, in our time, has become the very opposite of all this. It has become false, base, impure, crude, ugly and cheap. Because, as Christians, we live in this world but do not really belong here, the challenge comes to us, by the grace of God, to reverse the trend.

6. What We Live For

Someone once likened the world to a shop window where all the price tags had been shifted around, so that expensive things were priced cheaply, and things that were cheap were priced expensively. When we become Christians, we do begin to realize that we are living among people who have most of the true values inverted. This is particularly so in those sections of society where someone's worth is not assessed by what they are in themselves, but by what they possess or, more particularly, by the place they occupy in society.

The drive for status

'Well, he's *somebody*, you know', they say, implying, of course, that everyone else is nobody; 'He has a very important job', implying that everyone else's is unimportant; 'He went to a good school', implying that the others must be bad; 'He has letters after his name', comparing him with those who have not; 'He is very high up' in the Gas Board or the electronics world or what have you, implying that the rest are quite low down. It is this kind of off-the-cuff remark that often betrays someone's real sense of individual value and, equally, what they are aiming at in life themselves or, at least, where they would like to get to if they could.

In the last fifty years or so, there has been some quite incredible social levelling in England. The great gulf between rich and poor, high and low, has narrowed dramatically. However, in spite of this, we still have a society that has a pathetically high opinion of worldly honour and achievement, worldly position, power, class and influence. As a result, we live in a competitive and highly ambitious world, where folk who do not have status—which is the majority—are often tempted to join in the mad scramble to gain it for themselves.

We see this in the cut-throat business world in which many have to operate. We see it in what is, at times, the equally cut-throat academic world, for scholars have the same dose of human nature as the rest. We watch it going on in the political world, where it can be seen in the lust for power, whether in party politics or in union muscle. When you hear someone on TV boasting that they could 'bring them all out', and stop the country if they wanted to, it is nothing more than a crude expression of status.

But we do not have to go to the big names or the influential positions to see this. We can observe it in the petty one-upmanship among ordinary people. It might be the size of the house in which we live, or even the district where we live (some people are ultra-sensitive about having the 'right address'); it may have to do with the registration numbers of our cars, or where we went for our holiday last year; it may simply be that we have refurnished the lounge and that we want everyone to know.

Once again, our advertising friends are acutely aware of all this. We are actually sold some things because of the imaginary social status that goes with them. So the cheap car is pictured outside the mansion, or the cigarette is being smoked by the obvious socialite.

One of the particularly distressing trends of our time is that there are an increasing number of people who do not care very much what they have to do to gain status. It does not matter to them who they tread on, or how disloyal they might be, as long as they gain personal advancement. They call it, euphemistically, 'improving oneself', but you do not have to read much of the Bible to recognize this as a thin disguise for human pride and self-assertiveness.

Misdirected potential

What is most ironic about the whole business, is that human ambition and push are a sort of perverted virtue. It is the misuse of the potential built into man as he was created by God. When God made him in the first place, he gave him, as part of his dignity and distinctive difference from the rest, this sort of drive. Man was not made to stand still or to sit back. God delegated an authority to him. He was commissioned to exercise dominion over the rest of creation (Gen 1:28).

Because of this, we can say that we were made to exploit our opportunities. We were made to dream and to drive. We were given an initiative which can be seen in man's many and various achievements in design, exploration, development and creativity. Evidences of this are the great civilizations that have spread over the world at one time or another, or man's conquest of his environment, including space itself. It can all be attributed to man's inbuilt desire to get on and find out and overcome. And it is not all bad.

We can see the sad reverse of the situation when a nation goes into decline. A nation is perfectly capable of losing its nerve and sense of role, its collective ambition, if you like. Indeed, this is clearly the case with Britain since the Second World War.

The same sort of thing is true about the individual. It has been said that man's fundamental psychological needs are pleasure, security and *ambition*. When someone suffers from a depressive illness, ambition is something they lose. They do not feel like doing anything, especially anything creative. They lack the initiative they once had. They think they have nothing to live for. A person who loses his sense of purpose like this is ill. It is an abnormal condition, for God made man with drive and initiative.

Unfortunately, as we are living in a fallen world, all our natural potentials have been perverted to a greater or lesser degree towards sinful and selfish ends. What was originally a God-given sense of purpose, has been twisted into egocentricity. That is why you have a world that is running after status at any price.

What about the church?

If you talk to non-Christians in these terms, it will not be long before someone points out that those in the church can be just as bad. You do not have to read much church history to realize that there have been those within church organizations for whom prestige and influence were far more important than godliness. You only have to look at the splendours of something like the Vatican to see that. Church history has its dark side as well as its bright one, and we should be ready to confess that frankly.

What is more, although opportunities for this lust for
religious power are more limited today than they have
been in the past, the temptation is still with us. We can
see it within the denominational structures where there
are always those who like to have a say in what goes on.
There are still men who dream of high office or larger
congregations for their own sakes. Nor is this confined
to what we might call the mainline denominations.
There are plenty of breakaway groups, the structure of
which does not bear much scrutiny. Too often a man
has collected a following, and created his own little
empire, generally under the guise of 'spiritual over-
sight'. In fact, there are some men in the ministry who
are there because they need the following and the sense
of status that their position gives them, and which they
could not attain in any other profession.

But you can find the same temptation in ordinary,
common-or-garden service in the local fellowship. Why
do you serve? How would you feel if you were asked to
give up? We sometimes sing a hymn about church
members, a line of which runs, 'never from their office
move', and that is pathetically true in some situations.
There are workers in our churches who have long out-
lived their usefulness in the particular job that they do,
but who would never consider handing it on to someone else because of the status they would lose in the
process.

So there can be petty provinces of power even in the
local church. I once knew a lady who ruled the church
kitchen. It was her domain, and woe betide anyone
who even offered to help. It was seen as a threat to her
status—it was all so desperately sad. The world so often
gets into the church at this point. You do not need to be
Pope or Archbishop to be tempted to lust for power.

Personal advancement

It is easy to criticize the unconverted person whose life is dominated by ambition, but in the subtle atmosphere in which we all live, it is equally easy for Christians to begin to adopt the same attitude. How many Christian businessmen, for example, have been tempted to think more about getting to the top than about doing God's will? Sometimes it has meant sacrificing their personal scruples and principles in order to 'get on'. Jesus was tempted in that way too! In the wilderness, the devil showed him all the glory, riches and power of the world, and offered them to him, if only Christ would bow down and worship him (Mt 4:8). That kind of approach was cunning in the extreme. After all, in a way, that was why God's Son had come into the world, to re-establish his Lordship over all creation. After his death and resurrection, he could legitimately say, 'All authority has been given to me' (Mt 28:18). In effect, the devil was offering him a short-cut without the waiting or the suffering. But that way, it would have been without his Father's plan of salvation too, and much worse.

Ambition and status-seeking are not only male temptations. For example, wives can easily make social climbing a hobby, even though they profess to be Christians; the ladder of worldly status can become more important than seeking God's will for their lives. Or again, how many Christian parents entertain what are simply worldly ideas about what they want for their children in terms of career or marriage partners? When we say 'we only want the best for our children', are we sometimes really saying, 'We really want to maintain or improve our social status'?

How many Christians like to let us know what they

have done, or what they have achieved, or the position they hold? Or if they have little to boast about themselves, what members of their families have done? It is always sad to hear people boasting about their relatives and trying to bask in their status. My old pastor used to tell us that there were people who would always be ready to tell you that they were second cousin to a duke—although the duke himself would not own them!

When we examine our hearts and look into our motives, if we are really honest, who is faultless on this issue? How many of our deepest desires (however well disguised), how many of our plans (however well spiritualized), and how many of our reactions (when we are caught off our guard), betray worldly, carnal ambition? How many of us not only want to be approved by others, but wish to improve our status in their eyes? And how much do we sacrifice for all this?

Losing both ways

The kind of worldly ambition that we have been talking about leaves two sorts of Christians in its wake. There are those who have made it in this world. They are self-satisfied because they have arrived, and they do not mind letting you know about it. The other type are those who are disillusioned, discontented with their lot and frustrated—because they feel that they will never make it. Instead, they become bitter and envious of those who appear to have done better out of this world than they have.

Both kinds are compromised Christians, for the simple reason that worldly honour, worldly achievement, worldly preference and worldly status are just that. They belong to this world and to this time. You leave them all behind when you go. If you want a sobering exercise, read the obituary columns in the newspaper. See the impressive status that some have gained—only to leave it all behind. Sir So-and-So; the Honourable This; Lady That; long strings of honours or degrees or positions held or power wielded, and it has all *gone*.

Or go to the library, and you will discover that there are comparatively few people who have biographies that others actually want to read. What is more, in this age of debunking, there are those authors who delight to strip away the sham glory, and to paint their subject in the all-too-real colours of sordid human life. Sometimes those who have been honoured and favoured have achieved very little for anyone else but themselves. Their passing was no great loss to the world.

Back in Isaiah's time, the king of Babylon was a man like that. His personal pride knew no bounds. His power seemed irresistible. Whatever he wanted, he took for himself, and when he died, the whole world threw a party! (Is 14:1–21). And the pomp and power he had amassed during his lifetime? He left it all behind. And so will we.

A bit of honesty

How do you cope with this kind of temptation? Well, if you take the gospel seriously, worldly ambition should seem very thin. The basic Christian message has within it a good deal that will correct our spiritual short-sightedness, and bring things that really matter into sharper focus.

When you come to know Christ personally, you should come to an accurate assessment of yourself.

What are you really? What am I? In and of ourselves, we are sinners, and we are lost. We deserve absolutely nothing, and we never will. We are saved, rescued from our helpless condition, by grace. It is not our doing; it is entirely God's loving and merciful gift. 'By the grace of God I am what I am', wrote Paul, and even though he went on to say that he had used that grace well and wisely, achieving more than most, he added, 'it was not I, but the grace of God which is with me' (1 Cor 15:10).

If you have not come to that point, you have not come to the gospel, because that is where we must all begin— as sinners. From a Christian point of view, we accept humility as a virtue, but it is all because of the gospel. In the ancient world where the message was first preached, it was considered a vice. Then Jesus came, teaching his disciples, 'Blessed are the poor in spirit...' and 'Blessed are the meek...' (Mt 5:3, 5). Happy are those who have an accurate assessment of themselves in God's sight. If I have that, I can appreciate what Christ came to do for me.

But the gospel is not crushingly depressive, so that we spend our days bemoaning our sin and fallenness. It is equally by God's grace that I come into a new status, which is at once higher than anything this world can offer, and equally for all believers. I become an adopted child of God. This means that, however the world might assess me, and wherever the world might place me in its scale of values, I know my true worth to God. In Christ, by grace, I am his child. I am even a joint-heir with Christ himself, and so are all other Christians who are my brothers and sisters (Rom 8:17). We share the same privileges, irrespective of our worldly status.

Because of this, our church fellowships should be able to cross the otherwise unbridgeable divide between classes, cultures and colours. Background, intelligence, wealth, education, achievement, status mean nothing at the foot of the cross. There we stand together.

If we get a little depressed at times because this does not work out as it should, let us remember that it was a lesson that New Testament Christians had to learn too. James had some strong words for the wealthy who despised the poor in the assembly (James 2:1–7). He points out that it is often those who are poor in the world who are spiritually rich. Paul has a similar thing to say to his conceited friends at Corinth: 'Consider your call, brethren; not many of you were wise according to worldly standards, not many were powerful, not many were of noble birth' (1 Cor 1:26). God had not chosen them because of their earthly status, any more than he chose us for that reason. It was all grace. On that great day when we meet the Lord, he will not push aside the poor, the uneducated, the uncultured, the nobodies of this world in preference for those with rank and status. He will accept all alike as his children —and we should learn to do the same here and now.

Renewed ambition

The gospel can even transform ambition, and make it what it was originally intended to be. When you come to Christ, he gives you new ambition. This time it is not a scrambling after the honours of the world, but a longing to fulfil the purpose for which we were made. God made us for himself and for *his* glory. Hence, when we make our peace with him through Christ, his grace should then lead us into one overriding ambition to know him and to please him and to serve him.

Paul had to come this way. When writing to the church at Philippi, he gives us a glimpse of his pre-conversion ambitions. He had plenty of reason for what he calls 'confidence in the flesh', that is, in who he was and in what he had done. There would have been a good number in Jerusalem and Tarsus who would have said in envy, 'Look, there goes Paul.' And what does he say as a Christian? 'Whatever gain I had I counted as loss for the sake of Christ.' And what had come in its place? A longing to know him, to gain him, to be found in him, to be like him (Phil 3:4–11). Earlier in the letter he had summed up his new ambitions in a simple statement: 'For me to live is Christ' (1:21). In other words, for me, life means Christ now. That is the only legitimate ambition for a Christian.

Of course, as Paul pointed out, there is a negative side to this too. To share in Christ's resurrection life, he had also to share in his sufferings. He had to die to self in all its forms—self-interest, self-seeking, self-glory. It spelled the end of one-upmanship, social climbing and unbridled ambition. The challenge of discipleship means that, along with everything else we place on the altar, there must be our personal ambitions. That may mean letting go of cherished goals because you put Christ first.

This does not mean the end of all initiative and drive. On the contrary, the Lord, by the Holy Spirit, redirects and reharnesses that potential for himself. In fact, he makes more use of us than we could ever make of ourselves. There is an interesting phenomenon connected with evangelism and missionary work which is called 'conversion and lift'. What this means is that, when someone is converted, they often tend to better themselves and rise socially. It is sometimes quite a problem for those trying to maintain a Christian work in downtown areas. People come to Christ, 'get their act together'—and move out to something better! While this often causes frustration for inner-city ministers and missionaries who see their workers departing, it is none the less evidence of the fact that God reharnesses and redirects a life committed to him.

Christ and careers

The Lord does not necessarily take away your ambition, but he does change its direction. You are now doing what you do for him, and not just for yourself. I remember one young man who was an able pianist and who had come to Christ, talking over his attitude to his career with me. Professional music is one of those areas that demands complete dedication, and where very few make it to the top. He told me that, before he came to Christ, his one ambition was to do just that. After his conversion, for a while, it seemed as though the Lord had taken all that ambition away, but then he gave it back with a difference. He still wanted to succeed, but now he wanted to do it for the Lord.

There is a tremendous relief in knowing that, when you give your life to Christ, you commit your status to him as well. Get into his will, and he will take you to whatever position in society he thinks best, and you can be content there. The psalmist had it all worked out years ago: 'Not from the east or from the west, and not from the wilderness comes lifting up; but it is God who executes judgement, putting down one and lifting up another' (Ps 75:6–7). If God wants to 'raise you up', he will do the raising; and if he does not, whatever you do, do not try to raise yourself up! You can leave your status with him. You do not have to worry about it any more.

This is very important for those just starting out, who have to think about what career they must follow. How many have actually and deliberately asked, 'Lord, what do *you* want me to do?' It is not 'what do I want to do?' or 'what do my parents want me to do?', but 'what has God in mind for me?' If you are in his will, it does not really matter how the job rates in worldly terms. Perhaps it might be a good thing to remember that, as far as Scripture is concerned, there is no distinction between good jobs and bad jobs. To the Jews of Jesus' day, there was no difference between the white- and the blue-collar worker, between the clerical and the manual. That was a Greek distinction. For the Greeks, intellectual work was considered to be superior to manual work. But it is not biblical.

When God made his highest and best creation, man in his own image, he put him to work in a garden. There is a little couplet popularized at the time of the Peasants' Revolt:

> When Adam delved and Eve span,
> Who was then the gentleman?

This is why you find a man like Paul, with all his background and education, with his commission from the risen Christ as an apostle, earning his keep as a tent-maker when funds ran out. Forget those superficial worldly distinctions. Go to the Lord and ask him, 'Lord, what do you want me to do for you?'—not so much 'Lord, make me successful' as 'Lord, make me useful.

Put me in a job where you want me and where you can
use me for your glory.'

Saved to serve

Worldly ambition is essentially a form of self-seeking.
When we are obsessed with our own status, we are
simply serving ourselves. That is equally true if you
have ambitions for others—for husbands or for children
—in that their success in life reflects back on your
status. But putting ourselves first means putting others
in second place; others are there to serve us and our
ends. The gospel reverses all that.

Not only does the good news bring us to terms with
what we really are, renewing our ambitions, it makes
us into servants. Most of us can identify, unfortunately,
with James and John when they asked—or got their
mother to ask for them—for the prime places in the
kingdom (Mt 20:20–28). They did not know what they
were asking, for the way to spiritual greatness is the
way of suffering and the cross. Jesus had to tell them
that the way of the kingdom is not the way of the world,
where officials and petty tyrants rule over others. 'Whoever would be great among you must be your servant,
and whoever would be first among you must be slave of
all.' And if we ask why, that is the example he sets for
us. 'The Son of Man came not to be served but to serve,
and to give his life as a ransom for many.' He came as
the man for others, as someone who had the needs and
concerns of others at heart. He was at the disposal of
others, the Lord of All—even to the point where he was
prepared to die for them.

This is the One who calls us to follow him, and who
lays the mandate of service on each one of us. 'Great?

WHAT WE LIVE FOR   113

You want to be great? Then you must be servant and slave to others.' In one of the great crusades we have seen in this country in recent years, one man had the task of organizing all the stewarding. After delegating the work to this one and that, the job he gave himself was to stand at a door and tell the people to mind the step as they went in. He could have been sitting with the rest of the committee on the platform, under the lights and with the evangelist. But he had learned the lesson of serving others.

Are you really at the disposal of others, or do you resent the demands they make upon you, and their intrusion into your time and schemes? What is most important to you in this world? Is it the praise, the honour, the applause, the glitter, the envy of others? Or is it that 'Well done, good and faithful servant' when you finally see the Lord? It is not wrong to have ambition, drive and initiative. It is not wrong to want to go somewhere. That was the way God made us. But if you are a Christian, it is imperative that you have the right ambition.

7. How We Plan

I have a friend who has it all worked out. More than once he has told me what he is going to do, and when he is going to do it, and what he will do after that, and so on, for several years ahead. Understandably, his life so far has been a series of disappointments, because things do not always work out as we want them to, or as we plan them. That is why it is dangerous, not to say frustrating, to presume on what is going to happen. For presumption is just another sympton of the fallen age in which we live.

But that age is the same age in which New Testament Christians lived. That is why we have some very strong advice on the subject in James's letter (4:13–14). It may be that he had itinerant Jewish traders in mind. They travelled all around the Roman empire in those days, selling their wares and doing business. They had got it all worked out too. 'Today or tomorrow', they would say—the precise time—'we will go to such and such a town'—the particular city—'and spend a year there'—the exact length of the proposed stay—'and trade'—the specific business they would transact—'and get gain'—even the profit they would make. And James says that it is all presumptive: 'You do not know about tomorrow.'

You cannot presume on life. There is no saying what might happen, or even if you will be alive tomorrow. But that is exactly what the world does.

Worldly presumption

As we have seen, worldliness is not just a matter of what we do, but concerns the attitudes we adopt, and presumption is a far-reaching attitude to life. It means that we plan as though nothing could alter our plans. We assume that we are the masters of our own destiny. We arrange, and we organize, and we trust that events will run along the lines we have laid down. So we commonly come across people, like my friend, who will tell us that they are going to do this or that, take this job or that, go here or there. Once again, we see this in the plans that parents make for their youngsters. I once met a couple whose children were six and seven years old telling me about what they would do when they got to university! Young people themselves can easily fall into the trap: 'When I get to college...', they say, or 'When I get married...', or 'When I get out into my career....' Business planning today is little different from James's time. The successful businessman is the one who has it all worked out, and who pulls it off. The world congratulates people like that. It says that such people know where they are going, and what they want, but it is often entirely presumptive. As James reminds us, the time we call our own does not really belong to us at all. When we have everything set up we simply 'do not know about tomorrow'.

Life is uncertain

Underlying this whole attitude is the assumption that our life-span is guaranteed. You will remember that this was the fault of the Rich Fool, who pulled down his barns in order to build bigger ones. That was no mistake. The mistake came when he said to himself, 'Soul, you have ample goods laid up for many years.' The assumption was that he was not only going to live, but that it would be for a good, long time. And God said, 'Fool! This night your soul is required of you' (Lk 12:19–20). Not many years—now!

It is true that there are some people who are always telling you that they will be dead next year, but that is usually because they are neurotic and want attention. The average person assumes that they will live out the average life-span, and a bit more. People talk somewhat glibly about the biblical 'three-score years and ten', even though the insurance companies would put it at somewhat less than that these days. They presume on life, and they presume on health. In fact, they refuse to consider the hundred and one other possibilities that might wreck the whole scheme. Hence, they make their plans accordingly. They tell you what they will do in the next ten years, or what they have planned for their lengthy retirement. When they see others brought up short, they say, unconsciously if not openly, 'It could never happen to me.' They are presuming on life, whereas James reminds us that we do not even know about tomorrow, let alone next week, or next year. In fact, the only thing you can be absolutely sure about is that you are going to die sometime.

This uncertainty built into the nature of things is the reason why people get so shocked, hurt, frustrated and bitter when events do not work as they have planned them. They had it all set up, and providence decreed otherwise. If we were more realistic, we would admit that it is desperately easy for our plans to fall apart, and for our securities to crumble. This is one of the lessons we have had to learn the hard way through times of economic recession. You cannot assume business stability any more. You do not know where the market is going to go. Firms crash and all that you rely on can crash with them. No job is safe.

Over the years, one of the hardest jobs I have had has been to pastor mature people facing redundancy. It might have been a take-over by a larger company, or the firm simply folding up. However it happened, it left men in middle life and later—some of whom had been with the same company for years—feeling unwanted, lost and insecure. Home, lifestyle, family, pension arrangements, everything is affected, and sometimes almost overnight. The psychological blow is often devastating.

Other tragedies can strike families just as suddenly. An accident, a bereavement, children in trouble, unfaithfulness by one partner or the other, and the whole world seems to fall apart. I have met many who have reacted in bitterness and disappointment, and who have asked, 'Why should it happen to me? How could it happen to me?' If we were hard and unsympathetic, we might respond, 'Why not?' After all, that is life. It has happened to thousands of others. Why should you or I in particular be spared the sufferings, trials and disciplines that life doles out in unequal shares to everyone?

But their reaction betrays an underlying presumption about life. It says, loud and clear, 'I had it all worked

out. I don't deserve this.' You sometimes meet it when
someone has died somewhat prematurely. 'But he was
only fifty-two' or 'She was only forty-four'. That kind of
death may be tragic, but behind the common reaction
is the assumption that it is not quite fair; that we
deserve longer; that it is our right to live out what we
consider to be our full span of years. That kind of
reaction catches us—like most of our reactions—off our
guard. Whereas we can plan our actions, our reactions
often come unbidden, and when they do they sometimes betray that we are presuming on life, health and
the future.

Leaving God out

Modern man, as secular man, leaves God out of his
calculations, and that is often true in practice even
though his life might have more than a tinge of religion.
He generally has no sense of God's planning or purpose
for his life, in fact, he has little use of God except in
times of trouble and crisis. He has no real sense of
accountability to God, and no awareness that life is
God's gift. He forgets that the Lord gave, and that the
Lord can just as easily take away.

He has lost almost entirely a sense of what the old
folks used to call 'providence'. That was the conviction
that God was in control of all that happened, and that
God would supply our needs. In contrast, for all practical
purposes, modern man goes through life as though
God did not exist. He espouses the 'God is dead'
philosophy in the sense that the very idea of God as
someone we must trust, and someone to whom we
must answer, no longer has any significance for him. It
might have been a useful idea when the world was a

bigger, more frightening place than we know it to be now. In those days man needed a God to pray to and to trust in. But the scientists and experts have tamed the world, or at least have claimed to do so, and God has been shut out of the system.

That is why many, many people go through life with no real place for God or for the claims he might have on their lives. In practical, everyday terms, as we have said, they are atheists. They might live relatively decent, respectable lives, while at the same time ignoring God and presuming on life by taking it all for granted.

It is therefore curious to discover that modern man is still superstitious. It is rather illogical, but he still needs a sense of destiny, and in many ways he is very anxious about the future and what it might hold. A good number of people take far more notice of their horoscopes than they would like to admit. Luck may not be the boom trade that it is in the East, but it is still there in the background. Modern secular people still believe in lucky charms or lucky days or lucky mascots and the rest. When they do turn to religion it is often for a similar reason. Shakespeare read human nature well when he depicted the sailors on the sinking ship in *The Tempest* crying out, 'All lost—to prayers, to prayers'.

If that does not work, people become bitter and blame God for their lot. I knew a lady once who told me, somewhat illogically, that she did not believe in God, because God had let her mother die when she was young and needed her! What she meant was that God ought to have been there to do what she wanted when she wanted it done. She saw him as a God to be used— not a God to be worshipped, honoured and obeyed.

Another aspect of this widespread presumption is

that people get quite careless when it comes to God-given opportunities. The Bible tells us that God has not left himself without witness, even in an age when people have little practical place for him. Paul tells his friends that this was why pagan man was without excuse. God had shown enough about himself in what he had made, but people did not want to know. They suppressed the truth (Rom 1:18) and, in so doing, they took God's goodness for granted, for God was, in actual fact, giving them an opportunity of putting things right with him. The Jews were little better, even though they had God's written word, so Paul asks, 'Do you presume upon the riches of his kindness and forbearance and patience? Do you not know that God's kindness is meant to lead you to repentance?' (Rom 2:4).

Modern Western man has just as many opportunities of getting right with God. He has the Bible in his own language, and a church on almost every street corner. He has a long Christian tradition woven into the making of his society. He enjoys, through the social changes that this has brought about, many of the fringe blessings of the Christian gospel. But he does not want to know. He has no real time or place for God in his life, and his response to God's kindness is apathy. This is what we are up against when it comes to sharing the gospel. It is not that modern man does not have spiritual opportunities; he just could not care less about them, or about God.

Christians too?

Is it possible for this worldly attitude to get into the church and find a home among God's people? Unfortunately, it is. It is very easy for Christians to adopt a

similar attitude to life in practice—in spite of our prayers
and our professions. We also can presume on life, on
God, and on his providence. We see it in the self-confi-
dence with which some Christians take on life. It is not
always confidence in God. Rather, it is confidence in
their own abilities and their own expectations. They
have little idea that God might have a plan for them, so
they lay their own—and then ask God's blessing as an
afterthought.

It is all too easy to make our own plans, and then to
claim them to be divinely inspired. I sometimes upset
some of the students I teach when in response to their 'I
felt led...', I ask, 'Led by *what*?' What they mean, all
too often, is that they felt inclined to do something, and
that they then attributed their inclinations to God. The
problem then arises when God appears to change his
mind!

That is presumption. It may be spiritualized presumption, but it is still as worldly as the unbeliever's
attitude to life. A sure symptom is when a Christian
suffers disillusionment and disappointment over things
that do not work out as expected. Or when even professing Christians become bitter and resentful, and
start blaming God for what has happened. Actually,
when things go wrong, and when we cannot understand
what God is doing for us, faith really becomes faith. It
is comparatively easy to believe in God when all is well,
when you feel on top of things, and when you can
understand what is going on. But faith becomes real
faith when we do not feel like trusting God, and when
we can see no rhyme nor reason in our circumstances.
That is why Job's suffering was such a learning situation. He was left with nothing but faith.

When I was young I was given the advice, 'Never

doubt in the dark what you knew to be true in the light', and it has stood me in good stead many a time since. What is more, I have come to believe that, in order to mature our faith, God sometimes actually takes us into the dark; he knocks away all the props so that we might fall back on him. It is when we do not fall back into that submissive confidence, but into bitterness, regret, disillusionment and hurt, that we recognize that our faith was not real faith, but presumption after all. It becomes a moment of truth for us, when we realize that, instead of looking to him, and depending on him, and seeking his purpose for our lives, we had it all worked out. In other words, we were sharing the attitude of the age in which we live, the age that gets along without God.

Facing the future

Is there any answer to this? After all, our human nature is so twisted and self-deceiving that we are all prone to shift our faith from God to ourselves. Perhaps we had better start by being realists, for that is what Christians should be essentially, whatever others might say about them. We must acknowledge the brevity and insecurity of life. We must recognize that it is God's prerogative to give it or to take it away. This is something very fundamental in Scripture, that life is short and that God is the arbiter of human affairs.

Job prayed, 'Remember that my life is a breath' (7:7), a mere puff of air. For David, life was 'a few hand-breadths' and nothing in God's sight. 'Man goes about as a shadow' (Ps 39:5–6). Psalm 90 not only reminds us that we have but threescore years and ten here. It tells us that our lives are like a dream, or grass that is burned

up by the sun. 'Our years come to an end like a sigh...
they are soon gone, and we fly away.' Isaiah paints a
similar picture. 'All flesh', all humanity in its human
weakness, 'is grass, and all its beauty is like the flower
of the field. The grass withers, the flower fades' (Is
40:6–7). And, of course, this is the very truth that James
wanted to impress on his presumptuous friends: 'What
is your life? For you are a mist that appears for a little
time and then vanishes' (4:14).

I remember getting up early one autumn Sunday
morning, and going for a walk across the common near
our home. The mist was rising off the stream and the
damp grass as the sun soaked it up. And while I walked
and watched, it was soon all gone. That is James's
picture of life. It is as insubstantial as the morning mist.

In the teaching of Jesus and the apostles, there is
another complicating factor. It is not just that this life of
ours is not indefinitely extended; history itself will not
be indefinitely extended either. We are repeatedly told
in the New Testament, that one day—and it could be
any day—Christ is going to return. He is to break into
history once again, and when he does, he will cut short
the presumptive affairs of men and women.

Jesus told his friends that it will be like the days of the
Flood all over again. 'They ate, they drank, they married,
they were given in marriage, until Noah entered the
Ark and the flood came and destroyed them all' (Lk
17:27). Men and women will be going about their ordinary duties, and living as though life and time went on
for ever, presuming on life, on health and on the future
—and the Lord is going to break in and say, 'That's
enough!'

But the Christian ought to be aware of these things.
He should be realistic enough to recognize that this

world, this life, this age are not all that there is, and that what we experience here is merely a prelude. We are not here for long. We are just passing through. We have no fixed abode in this world. So whether this life of ours or the age itself comes to an end, we should be ready for it.

Using our options

All this does not mean that we live this life irresponsibly. On the contrary, the Christian takes his responsibilities very seriously. In one of his plays, George Bernard Shaw tried to make out that the longer you lived, the more careful you became, and that if we knew we would live for a long time, we would be far more responsible. That simply is not the way in which human nature works. Most of us perform best under pressure. When I am writing, the fact that the publisher gives me a deadline is an excellent stimulus to getting on with the job. And we all have a deadline to meet.

Some years ago, one of my church officers fell ill and the doctors told him that he had about six months to live. Actually he lived for about eighteen, and they were eighteen months of enormously effective testimony. How that man organized his days! How he was prepared to witness and to share his faith! When I talked with him, he told me of his new sense of purpose in living, because he knew he did not have long, and, as I listened, I realized that we are all like that. Maybe the doctor has not said to us, 'You have another twenty-five years' or 'You have another two', but we are all in this condition. We are all dying men and women.

As we have seen, Psalm 90 dwells on this fact, and it could be somewhat depressive had not the Psalmist drawn out the spiritual lessons. Having told us to be realists about the brevity of this life, he prays, 'So teach us to number our days that we may get a heart of wisdom' (Ps 90:12). The fact that we do not have long should make us live all the more responsibly.

Finding God's plan

Christians are not only realists about this life, they recognize God's meaning and purpose in the short time we have here. The Bible teaches that we are not here simply to enjoy this life, or even to survive this life. In the wisdom of God, we are here on trial. This life is a brief probationary period. 'It is appointed for man to die once, and after that comes judgement' (Heb 9:27). This implies that it is also appointed for man to live once with judgement in mind. It is this life and what we have done in this life that is going to count on the judgement day.

That is no hardship for the truly converted person. In fact, it is a great discovery, that the ages have over-lapped, and that we can already experience something of the life to come. As far as salvation is concerned, we are already the other side of the grave and judgement, even though we will still have to answer for the service we have put in, and for the way in which we have used our opportunities here and now.

This is what the parable of the Pounds is all about. The nobleman called his servants, gave them their money, and said, 'Trade...till I come' (Lk 19:13). And when he returned, they all rendered an account of their trading. This life, this age as long as it lasts, is the trial period when we can learn to trust and prove the Lord, as well as serve him faithfully. It will come to an end sooner or later, but the question is not how long this will be, but how well we live; how well, that is, we use our spiritual opportunities here and now.

In my student days I was sent from college one week-end to conduct the services in a little church out in the country. I stayed with three old ladies in a mansion full of relics which was quite eerie. However, the father of the eldest, who had built the house, had been well involved in the early developments of the China Inland Mission. So, on Sunday afternoon, as we politely drank tea together, she pulled out an old leather-bound visitors' book for me to see. There was the great Hudson Taylor's signature, together with a verse of Scripture, and a little couplet that has remained with me ever since:

> Only one life, 'twill soon be passed;
> Only what's done for Jesus will last.

For that is what life is all about for Christians. It is a matter of finding and fulfilling God's plan for our lives.

I think that was one of the most thrilling discoveries I ever made as a young Christian: the fact that God had a purpose for my life. He had something for me to do, something for me to be, and somewhere for me to go. Paul reminds us that God has prepared beforehand the things he wants us to do for him (Eph 2:10). That is also why James tells his friends that, instead of presuming on time and life, they ought rather to say, 'If the Lord wills, we shall live and do this or that' (4:15). God's will for me should be my prime concern, whether my life is short or long.

In practice, it means taking each day as an unrepeat-able opportunity. Get hold of this fact. Time is our most precious commodity. We can lose money and make it again. But when time is gone, it has gone, and it has gone for ever. Each day is a precious gift. We must not presume on it, but then neither must we waste it. We must take it gratefully from our Father's hand, and use it for him.

This will mean walking closely with him, subjecting our wills to his. There has been a great deal said and written about guidance, but it can never be understood apart from a daily walk with God. As we let the Lord into each aspect of every day, practising his presence in the ordinary things of life, we begin to pick up the thread of his purpose for us. The starting point for guidance is when we get into step with God each day.

Father knows best

It will also mean that we can refuse to be disappointed if things do not work out as planned. We must plan ahead. That is part of our stewardship. But we must be ready to allow God to change our plans if he so wishes. I had a most godly church secretary when I began in the ministry. He was very old and I was very young, but we hit it off well together. It was not an easy church, and things did not always work out as we wanted them to. It was then that he would look at me in his wise old way and say, 'Well, pastor, Father knows best.'

If God is your heavenly Father, and if he is also sovereign in his universe, then you can begin to take every circumstance, every issue, every difficulty and every problem that comes your way from a Father's hand. It is that way that you begin to prove that 'in everything God works for good with those who love him' (Rom 8:28). 'Everything' means that there are no accidents where God is concerned, but it also means that we begin to experience a good number of coincidences. In fact, although coincidences did occur occasionally before I was converted, afterwards they became commonplace. I discovered that so many other tributaries fed into the stream of God's will for my life. God, my heavenly Father, was sovereign even in the details of daily living. He could set up the circumstances of each day. He could organize the work I had to do, and the people I had to meet, and the difficulties I had to encounter. What is more, I could accept them all confidently from a Father's hand.

All I had to do was to co-operate with him by staying in the centre of his will for me. I must not lag behind and be slow in obeying him, but then neither must I run ahead, and presume on his will for me. The Psalmist got it right: 'Keep back thy servant also from presumptuous sins; let them not have dominion over me' (Ps 19:13). In other words, prevent me from running ahead, like a little child running ahead of its mother in a crowd, and getting itself lost. Of course we have to think ahead. Life demands that, but we do it with this proviso. As James puts it, 'If the Lord will . . . we shall do this or that' (4:15).

In the old days, some folk were very fond of putting 'DV' after everything they suggested. 'The meeting will be held on April 18th, DV'; 'I will see you on Sunday, DV.' DV is short for the Latin, *Deo volente*, which means 'God willing'. I think the phrase became a bit trite, but I do hope that we still believe the heart of it. I do hope that we recognize that God's providence—the fact that God is in control and that God will supply—is the antidote for worldly presumption.

Thy way, not mine, O Lord,
However dark it be!
Lead me by Thine own hand,
Choose out the path for me.
Horatius Bonar

8. The Things We Enjoy

There can be no disputing that we are a pleasure-seeking generation, and some would say, 'Why not?' All work and no play makes Jack a dull boy. Surely we need some sort of escape from the pressing responsibilities of life? One of the stock criticisms of the church over the years has been that it has been unreasonably kill-joy both in its attitudes and in its message. The world tells Christians that they are afraid to enjoy themselves. In fact one of the standard excuses for not listening to the gospel message is that becoming a Christian means giving up so many enjoyable things. The typical caricature of the Christian is that of a dour, long-faced and joyless individual, who wants to impose the same sort of gloom on others.

On the debit side, there have been and still are Christians who give the impression that Christian living is a pretty grim affair. They regularly confess themselves to be miserable sinners—and they are! They are the sort of people who seem to want all their hymns in the minor key, and for whom laughter in church is sacrilegious. Life, for them, is far too serious a business to enjoy. Hence it looks as though we are dealing with a cluster of misunderstandings both inside and outside the church. Let us try and put the record straight.

Enjoy yourselves!

Let us start by saying that pleasure, or leisure, or relaxation, or recreation—which are all the same group of ideas—are built-in needs as far as man is concerned. This was the way God made us. All work and no play *does* make Jack—and Jill too—a very dull person. That is just as true for those who make no claims to being Christians, but who are so busy and so involved that they never have time to relax.

God did not design us to be working all the time. God gave us, and built into our human constitution, the need for mental and physical escape. Remember that it was the Lord who established the original day of rest which became part of the Ten Commandments (Ex 20:8–11). In the first place, that one day in seven was meant to be not just an opportunity for worship, but also a time for rest, recreation and relaxation. It has been misinterpreted over the years, but originally it was for our benefit and our good. As Jesus said, 'The sabbath was made for man' (Mk 2:27).

Because Jesus was fully human, he felt the need for a break at times, just as we do. In the middle of a very busy ministry when, we are told, 'they had no leisure even to eat', Jesus said to his friends, 'Come away by yourselves to a lonely place, and rest a while' (Mk 6:31). In other words, 'Let's have a day off. Let's get away and take time out.' If Jesus needed that, so do we.

It is no mistake that one of the Bible pictures of heaven is that of rest (2 Thess 1:7). It was the word they used when they unstrung their bows by relaxing the tension on the string. When we get to glory, the strain and pressure and toil of this life will fall away, and we should be getting a glimpse of that here and now. It is not that the Bible hallows laziness; the rest it describes is obviously rest after labour. Sloth, in the Scriptures, is a sin, but relaxation is not.

This is something tense and busy people need to be taught today. God made us with a need for regular recreation, and provided for us, in the world that he made, so many good things that are pleasurable and enjoyable in themselves. When pointing Timothy away from the uncertain riches of this world, Paul also tells him that 'God ... richly furnishes us with everything to enjoy' (1 Tim 6:17). When he used that word 'everything', he meant it. God not only created us with a capacity for enjoyment, he made an enjoyable world for us to live in. In other words, it was God's original intention that we should go through life enjoying it.

It is not always easy to see what the preacher in Ecclesiastes was driving at in his subtle analysis of human life, but on this issue he is plain. 'There is nothing better for a man than that he should eat and drink, and find enjoyment in his toil. This also, I saw, is from the hand of God' (Eccles 2:24). Men and women were not meant to go through life sorry that they were ever born, and longing for the grave. God made a good and pleasurable world for us to live in and enjoy. That is why, incidentally, he gave man a sense of humour and the power to laugh. Someone who cannot do this is missing out in life.

Leisure, pleasure, joy, humour, relaxation—all these things are legitimate and necessary, and part of God's intention for his creatures. They are some of God's good gifts to us. What has happened is that, like so many of God's gifts, we have spoiled, corrupted and misused them. What was originally entirely for our good has been used by Satan to become a snare and a bondage.

A way out?

Pleasure nowadays is a highly ambiguous term. That is why we are having difficulty in discussing it. It has been distorted from its original purpose in a number of ways. For some it has become a way of escape. What was originally intended to be temporary release and recreation has become a means of escaping the harsh realities of life. The fantasy world of modern pleasures is where men and women often run to in order to get away from the responsibilities, duties and challenges of daily living. This is understandable, of course, if they have no God to run to. The difference, when you run to God for help and relief, is that he puts you right, refreshes you, and then sends you back with new strength and intention. For the world, however, pleasure is simply a way of forgetting.

That is why, for many of our generation in the West, pleasure has become a drug and like every addiction, it demands a continued and increasing supply. So people live for the latest film, or another night out, or the next drink. Man without God, for all his bravado and boasted independence, is lost in a bewildering and vast world from which he seeks some kind of escape. This is why pleasure is such big business in our time, and why pleasure-seeking in one form or another has taken on such huge proportions. Not only do people exploit and distort the things God originally gave us to enjoy, they also hunt around for synthetic pleasures that offer a way out, and that are so short term in their satisfaction. It seems ironic that, when the effects wear off, people are more miserable than they were before.

I used to have morning coffee in a café in a busy London street. Sitting behind the plate-glass window provided an ideal vantage point from which to study humanity as it passed by outside. Very seldom did I ever see anyone smiling or happy. Try it for yourself. Look at the faces of the crowds in any city street, and you may well conclude with me that we are a pretty miserable generation.

Forbidden attractions

But man is not only lost, he is also fallen. He possesses a twisted, sinful human nature that perverts anything it comes into contact with. This is why man as we know him not only delights in legitimately pleasurable things, he also takes pleasure in evil. As morally endowed creatures, pleasure-seeking men and women discover that strange phenomenon which we call the attraction of the forbidden. There is something about what we should not or ought not to be doing that appeals to our corrupt human nature.

The apostle Paul tells us how he discovered this in his own experience (Rom 7:7–12). As a Jew, he had been taught to have respect for God's Law. In fact, along with many in his generation, he believed that by trying hard to keep it, he could save himself. However, when he tried to keep to the Law, he learned something rather alarming about himself. This was that the Law not only showed him what right and wrong were, it actually provoked something in him into rebellion, something he calls 'sin'. Paul is writing as a Christian now, and is giving us a very clear and honest insight into human nature. No Jew would have ever said that about God's Law; it would have been disrespectful to say the least. Paul agrees that God's Law is 'holy, and the commandment is holy and just and good', but the problem lies in the fact that, although the Law is good, we are bad. That is why we need more than forgiveness. We need the potential to deal with the sin principle within our natures.

Several centuries later, the theologian Augustine illustrated the same point in his famous *Confessions*. He tells the story about his boyhood, when he and his friends went scrumping, and stripped a neighbour's pear tree of all its pears. It was not because they wanted to eat them all—actually they dumped most of them—it was because of the sheer pleasure of doing what was forbidden.

It is this that sets the pattern for a great deal of worldly pleasure, and that has made Christians over the years say that a lot of it is far from innocent. We see it today in the sort of films that are made, and the sort of books that are written, and the sort of shows that are staged. What is selling in the entertainment world is often what appeals to our lower natures. It is the sensuality, or the horror, or the unnatural crime, or the violence that draws crowds at the box office or raises the TV viewing ratings. It often goes by the euphemistic name of 'adult entertainment', but only if 'adult' means having a corrupted nature, is that a fair description.

Those who go and see such shows, or read such books, might not go to the same lengths themselves in their own behaviour, but they are taking pleasure in evil. They are sinning at second-hand, although sometimes that is the first step towards sinning at first-hand. It is one of the ways in which Satan undermines our defences and lowers our standards. Paul describes this condition: 'Though they know God's decree that those who do such things deserve to die, they not only do them, but approve those who practise them' (Rom 1:32).

Approval of evil in terms of enjoying what is evil is just as bad as being involved in it yourself. Unfortunately, you run that risk with so much that passes as pleasure nowadays.

Pleasure as God

An equally disturbing aspect of modern, Western life is that, for many, pleasure-seeking has become obsessional. It would not be too much to say that with some people it has become a religion. Often they are only trying to fill that great gap in lives lived without God. The same Augustine also wrote, 'You have made us for yourself, and our hearts are restless till they find their rest in you.' As someone once put it, there is a God-shaped blank in everyone's life. If God does not fill it, we have to try to fill it with something else, and for many today that something is pleasure.

They just *live* for the evening, when they can go out on the town; they *live* for the weekend. Work is just a means to that end. There is little job satisfaction, and often very little idea that work might be pleasurable and fulfilling. Instead, people live for the synthetic pleasures that are available out of working hours. It is the sort of thing that Paul meant when he spoke of people in his own day who were 'slaves to various passions and pleasures' (Tit 3:3). They had become obsessive for them. They served them as religiously as they ought to have been serving God.

He told Timothy that this was a symptom of the days before Christ's return. Not only will moral disorder be commonplace, men and women will be 'lovers of pleasure rather than lovers of God' (2 Tim 3:4). Pleasure will take God's place. People will live for it, just as they are living for it today in the West.

And the church?

Can the world penetrate the church at this level? Perhaps Christians have been so aware of the dangers over the years that they have generally run to the opposite extreme, and gained their somewhat sombre reputation. And yet, as we have seen, living in any age makes us susceptible to the attitudes all around us, and the current attitude to pleasure is no exception. I can assume, just as easily as unbelievers, that pleasure is a justifiable *end* in life. I can convince myself that I am here *primarily* to enjoy myself. Perhaps this is another reason why the hard demands of exclusive discipleship are not as popular in our churches as they ought to be. Perhaps this is why Christians today find it difficult to face suffering and loss as well as their forefathers did.

At a lower level, it can spill over into what we do together as Christians. Preachers can be assessed by the number of laughs they can raise. Worship can be viewed as another form of entertainment. Instead of coming to a service offering to God worship and ourselves, as well as offering fellowship to others, we come wanting to know what we can get out of it. A 'good service' can become one that makes us feel good.

Out of church it is also very easy for us individually to let human nature off the leash when it comes to our private entertainment. So we watch that TV programme, or go off to see that play, or sit down to read that novel without being honest enough to admit that we are sharing the world's pleasure in evil. Before we know where we are, we have lowered our standards, and taken in things not fit for Christian consumption. It is a fallacy to describe something as being 'as ugly as sin'. Sin is generally very attractive to our old human natures, and that is why, all too often, the things that amuse the world amuse us too.

That kind of involvement ruins our witness, of course. The salt loses its taste and the light is blotted out when we join in with the rest and do what they do—even when we do it with the excuse that we are 'witnessing' to them. They see through that one even if we do not. It also stunts our spiritual growth. As we have seen, when Jesus explained the parable of the Sower, he likened the thorns to 'the cares, the riches and the *pleasures* of life', which choke the life out of the seed and stop the fruit maturing (Lk 8:14).

As we have noted, in the 1980s we are seeing something of a swing away from the legalism of the 1950s in our churches. The negative image of Christian living has been seen to be both unbiblical and unsatisfying. Yet there was a truth highlighted by the old approach that we are in danger of losing if we are not careful. When we become Christians, there *are* some things that are totally incompatible with our new commitment. There are some things which *do* have to go if Jesus is going to be Lord in our lives. They include certain pleasures that are more than dubious. If we are honest, they are plain sinful, or they open us wide to temptation. Is that hard? Not when you remember that for whatever he takes away, the Lord always gives far more back in compensation.

Solid joys

If God created us with a constitutional need for enjoyment, it follows that God alone is able to completely satisfy it, and this is what he offers to do through the gospel. That is why 'joy' is a frequent word in the New Testament, as are 'peace' and 'rest'. The Christian has something to be happy about for, when he comes to Christ, God begins to remake him in the original design. He brings us back into fellowship with himself, and the great gap in our lives is filled—for the first time. That is why Jesus could appeal to the crowds who were labouring under the wearying yoke of religious legalism, 'Come to me all who labour and are heavy laden, and I will give you rest. Take my yoke upon you and learn of me . . . and you will find rest for your souls' (Mt 11:28–29).

I was once asked to speak at a college Christian Union on the title 'Is Christianity Escapism?', and I had to admit that for some people it was. They ran away from real life into religion. But then I went on to point out that there was a perfectly legitimate escapism as well. The Bible tells us that we need to escape from what we are heading for, and that we can do so by running away—to God. When we do that we find a rest, a joy and a peace that answers to the deepest needs of our human make-up. That is the message of the New Testament.

Take Paul's statement in Chapter 5 of Romans. We not only know peace with God as Christians, we also rejoice in the confidence of sharing his glory one day. But more than that. We can even rejoice, as Christians, in our *sufferings*, in the disciplines of life, its adverse circumstances. Why? Because we know that, if God is in charge, these things must be working out his purposes for us here and now. In these verses Paul points out that the pressures of life actually contribute to our spiritual growth and progress.

No wonder non-Christians cannot understand

Christians. Who ever dreamed of rejoicing over one's sufferings? And yet they were like that in the beginning. Do you remember the story of Paul and Silas at Philippi? They had been falsely accused, attacked by a crowd, beaten with rods, thrown into the inner prison and, for extra security, had their feet put in the stocks. What were they doing at midnight? Praying and singing hymns to God—which was somewhat unnatural in the circumstances! But they believed that God was in control and that they were suffering for Christ—and God gave them a joy that transcended stocks and prison and everything else.

In the early days of the Salvation Army the movement was receiving a good deal of criticism nationally, so a reporter went along to one of their meetings to see what went on. While standing at the door watching the people going in, he noticed a Salvationist couple coming along with their little boy. The lad slipped on the step, grazed his knee and burst into tears. 'Say "Hallelujah", son', said his father. 'Hallelujah, daddy', the little boy tearfully replied—and the newspaper headline next day was, *The religion that can say Hallelujah through its tears!* That is our religion. That is Christianity.

And the secret? Read Paul's letter to Philippi that picks up the theme of joy again and again. The apostle sums it up: 'Rejoice in the Lord always, and again I will say, rejoice' (4:4). That is the secret. We do not only rejoice in our circumstances, in the variable happenings of life which may be pleasant or otherwise. We rejoice in Christ.

Human love is fickle. It ebbs and flows, and sometimes the people we love let us down. But the Lord is constant. He is always there, and he is always the same. He is independent of circumstances. So our happiness is no longer tied to the chance happenings of life. It is centred in One who loved us and gave himself for us.

They learned this lesson in Old Testament times first. We see it well illustrated for us in the little prophecy of Habakkuk. All kinds of dreadful things were happening to his people, which he could not understand, and in which he simply had to learn to trust God. There was nothing in his circumstances to make him at all cheerful, but he ends with a triumphant statement of faith and praise (3:17–18):

> Though the fig-tree do not blossom,
>   nor fruit be on the vines,
> the produce of the olive fail,
>   and the fields yield no food,
> the flock be cut off from the fold
>   and there be no herd in the stalls,
> yet I will rejoice in the Lord,
>   I will joy in the God of my salvation.

What the prophet is saying is, 'Let it all come, Lord. I've still got you, and I can rejoice in you.'

When you have that kind of joy, the pleasures of the world seem rather flat. I remember being invited to a sherry party once with a group of non-Christians. Our generous hostess had seen to it that there was plenty of drink for everyone (and even a jug of orange juice for me!). It was a pleasant enough evening with the usual small talk, but it never really got going. A little later we had a get-together in our own home for half a dozen or so Christians, and the whole thing simply took off—on grapefruit juice! The difference? When you get a crowd of Christians together, they almost spontaneously begin to enjoy themselves. It is because they have the Lord in their hearts and they are rejoicing in him—or at least, they should be. As the Psalmist put it, 'In his presence there is fulness of joy; at his right hand there are pleasures for evermore'(Ps 16:11).

While we are on the subject, a great deal has been said about alcohol in the context of worldliness in the past, to the point where, for some, drinking is a sin. Although drunkenness is certainly described in that way in the Bible, drink as such is neutral. Jesus both drank and turned water into the best wine. What I have discovered, however, is that when it comes to enjoying yourself, as a Christian I really have no need for it. The Lord has given me a joy and a satisfaction that is worlds apart from joy out of a bottle. And when drink becomes a social issue, as it has done in the West, I find it no hardship to go without it for the sake of my 'weaker brother'. This is no doubt what Paul had in mind when he contrasted being drunk with wine and being filled with the Spirit (Eph 5:18). Perhaps if we knew the Lord as we ought, we would get drink into its proper perspective, and we would find ourselves less dependent on other synthetic pleasures too.

How to be happy

The wonderful truth is that, when you come to know Christ, he not only gives you a new joy in himself, he gives you a new capacity for enjoying yourself—because he gives you a new capacity for living. When you become a Christian, you should enjoy your work and not only your recreation times, for everything should be touched and coloured by the new satisfaction that you have in the Lord Jesus Christ. This means that you can enjoy all God's gifts as you never did before.

You can read a good book to his glory, or play a game of football to his glory. It is true that as a Christian you have a new sense of stewardship. This means that you may have to think twice before doing some things which are so expensive that they take money that ought to be spent on other things. But remember that stewardship cuts both ways. It not only means that we must not waste things; it also means that we must use them and employ them.

Besides giving you spiritual life, God has also given you minds and bodies, health and energy and interests. God wants you to be a complete person, for he is re-creating you in his own image. Because of this, the Christian is as responsible to God for his leisure time as for his working time. That is why we should get very concerned about the Christian who is so busy that he never takes any time off. There are some who, when not at work, are out employed in Christian activities to the exclusion of everything else. They have somehow got it into their heads that they must be working all the time if they are going to honour Christ. We have students who work like that, and whom we have to stop working! We have to say, 'For goodness' sake, go and have a game of squash', 'Go for a swim', or 'Go for a walk on the common'. Taking time out is as important as spending time in the library.

I rarely read women's magazines, but a little time ago an article in one that belonged to my wife caught my eye. It was written by a doctor and entitled 'How to keep your man alive'. Naturally I was interested to see what she was being advised to do. One of the things that struck me was the insistence that this unknown doctor put on leisure time. 'Make sure', he wrote, 'he has a hobby'. In other words, make sure he takes time out to relax.

Christian gloom

What about those who feel guilty if they are not either working in their full-time employment, or engaged in some specifically Christian activity? These are the ones who feel guilty if they sit down with a book, or go out for a run, or take time off in some form or other. If you fall into that category, may I suggest that you are simply too busy and that you may be something of a workaholic? It is both unnatural and unbiblical. God never meant you to be like that, and he never meant you to neglect the many good things of life that he gave you to enjoy. There are even Christians who have got to the point where they feel that, if they are enjoying something, then it cannot be God's will. God's purpose, for them, must be something unpleasant, like medicine which they think ought to taste nasty if it is going to do any good.

Where did the idea of Christian gloom come from? Curiously enough, we picked the idea up from the Greeks once again. They argued that matter was evil and spirit was good, and they sometimes went on to say that it was unimportant what you did with your body. So some were as permissive as any modern person, and a good deal more so. Others, starting from the same point, came to the opposite conclusion; they said that you have to discipline your body and its appetites rigidly and strictly.

Whereas Christians saw the obvious evil in the first approach, the second seemed to be more along the lines of New Testament self-denial. This is what developed into the ascetic traditions of the monastic movement that have persisted until modern times. Christianity must be sober. Appetites must be bridled and checked.

Self must be put down by rigorous discipline.

But this is also a perverted half-truth. Read the story of Jesus. He was no ascetic, and we are called to follow him, not some misanthropic Greek. He went about doing good, bringing joy and spreading happiness and, by his Spirit, he still does the same today.

There are certain disciplines that we accept. There are things that have to go. There are certain checks that Christ brings to bear upon our lives. But the positive side, the life he gives back in return, is far richer than anything we could possibly construct for ourselves. It would be a sin not to enjoy it. The familiar chorus is surely correct that says,

> Thank you for pleasure and enjoyment,
>   Thank you for every heartfelt joy.
> Thank you for all that makes me happy,
>   And for melody.

Christ has called us to 'the life that is life indeed' (1 Tim 6:19), the complete and fulfilled life that only he can give us. Let us show the world what enjoyment really is!

9. What Is At Stake?

Reading this book, some may have felt that I have been taking things a bit too far. Why all this talk about the world and its influence on the Christian? Surely we ought to accept the world as it is, and get on with the job of trying to improve it? But this would be to overlook the very sobering teaching of Christ and his followers about the world, and about its fate.

World under judgement

Because God is a just God as well as a sovereign one, he is not going to allow the rebellious situation in the world to persist for ever. Sooner or later, he is going to wind up the present system, and bring this evil age to a conclusion. We have more than one reference in the New Testament to the judgement of the world, and of its diabolical leadership (Jn 12:31; 16:11; Rom 3:6). They are doomed to 'pass away' (1 Cor 2:6). Even the physical world was not built to last. It too will come to an end at the coming of Christ (2 Pet 3:10–12).

When we talk about Christian realities, we are not playing games. This is a matter of life and death. The sinful, fallen world, out of which we have been saved, is going to hell, as surely as those outside the Ark were all swept away by the Flood. When Paul advises his Corinthian friends about getting their church life sorted out and brought under the discipline of Christ, it was 'that we might not be condemned along with the world' (1 Cor 11:32).

In our rush to make the gospel palatable and up to date, we have often overlooked the harsh realities that underlie it. Man *is* fallen and sinful. God's just judgement on sin *is* eternal death. That is what we all deserve and, apart from Jesus Christ, there is no escaping that destiny. You did not become a Christian merely because it did you good, or because you feel better as a result. You did it for the same reason that you would jump out of the way of an oncoming train, or throw yourself out of a blazing building. The evangelist's call should not be, 'Come to Jesus for a great time', but rather, 'Save yourselves from this crooked generation' (Acts 2:40).

In the modern world we live under the shadow of the Bomb. Sooner or later, we fear, some idiot is going to press the button, and all that we know as civilization will be brought to an end. Actually, we are living in a far greater peril than that. Any time, any day now, Jesus Christ is going to break in on this fallen and corrupt situation as Lord and as Judge. The day of opportunity will be over. We will all stand before his judgement seat. On that day you will either be found in the Ark or in the water; you will either be saved, or lost.

The Christian life is a marvellous life. It is a full life, a life packed with possibilities here and now, but, most important, it is the life of the age to come begun here and now. By the Holy Spirit we anticipate the Judgement Day, and bring it forward in our experience. We feel it in the keenness of conviction of sin, when we see sin to be the horrible thing that it is. We know what it is to die—with Christ—and we begin to prove his resurrection life. But many will not. Make sure you are not among them.

A pure bride

More than once in the New Testament, the church is described, as Israel was of old, as a wife or bride. Christ is the husband, who loves his people as deeply as a lover longs for his spouse. It follows that the only bride worthy of the name must be pure and committed to her heavenly partner. He wants a church 'without spot or wrinkle or any such thing', a church that is 'holy and without blemish' (Eph 5:27). Anything less than that, as they were told in the Old Testament, is spiritual adultery.

Put another way, God wants 'a people for his possession' (1 Pet 2:9), exclusively belonging to him. No wonder James reminds us that 'friendship with the world is enmity with God' (Jas 4:4), and John tells us that 'if anyone loves the world, love for the Father is not in him' (1 Jn 2:15). Whether we like it or not, there is a necessary dividing line between God's people and the rest, if we are to be God's people at all. When it is there, we honour him—and the world hates us (Jn 15:18–19; 17:14–15). When it is absent, we merge with the rest and our witness is lost.

The church only has a message for the world and a ministry to it when she is significantly different from the world. Paul reminded the Philippians that, as they co-operated with the God who was at work in their lives, they would be his children 'without blemish in the midst of a crooked and perverse generation, among whom you shine as lights in the world, holding fast the word of life' (Phil 2:14–16). The trendy, with-it Christian, who goes along with the rest in attitude and behaviour 'in order to win them', has simply missed out. The light is doused; the salt has become tasteless and useless.

That is equally true of the church at large when it gives the outsider the impression of being no more than a club with a religious flavour. We lose our cutting edge when, in practice, we are no different from the world. We have nothing distinctive to offer. We are irrelevant to a lost generation.

Come out; be separate!

I suppose that in one sense it is a comfort to know that the apostles faced the same sort of problems, although in different ways. New Testament churches were far from perfect, as the bulk of the New Testament letters testify. They too had to be warned about the dangers, and challenged with the issues.

We find one of the most comprehensive appeals when Paul wrote to the church at Corinth, and it is well worth citing again:

> Do not be mismated with unbelievers. For what partnership have righteousness and iniquity? Or what fellowship has light with darkness? What accord has Christ with Belial [that is, the devil]? Or what has a believer in common with an unbeliever? What agreement has the temple of God with idols? For we are the temple of the living God; as God said, 'I will live in them and move among them, and I will be their God, and they shall be my people. Therefore come out from them, and be separate from them,' says the Lord,

'and touch nothing unclean; then I will be a father to you, and you shall be my sons and daughters,' says the Lord Almighty. Since we have these promises, beloved, let us cleanse ourselves from every defilement of body and spirit, and make holiness perfect in the fear of God. [2 Cor 6:14–7:1.]

As you can see, there are plenty of attached promises for us to prove. If we want God's blessing in our lives and in our churches, then this is the way. Revival begins when God's people begin to take him seriously.

If the demands he makes seem hard to meet, and if there are things we dearly love that need to go, remember why we do it. No one would have done more, or given up more, or suffered more, for us than Jesus. If it seems hard to let those things go, think about the cross, 'by which', as Paul wrote elsewhere, 'the world has been crucified to me, and I to the world' (Gal 6:14).

I suppose that it is working in a co-educational college that gives me plenty of first-hand experience of youngsters falling in love with one another, but I never fail to be amazed at what it does for people. All kinds of things that he—or she—did before now become unimportant somehow. Instead, both cultivate a whole new set of interests which they share with one another. The psychologists call it 'the expulsive power of a new affection'. If you feel that someone is worth it, there are no lengths to which you will not go in order to please them.

Is Christ worth it? When faced with the glitter and sham of the world, all its short-lived pleasures and tissue-thin securities, isn't it worth trading for him? If you are still regretting what you might have to give up, it is plain that you have never really experienced what it is to love him, and to be loved by him.